The

RICHEST
MAN
in
NEW
BABYLON

An Inspirational Story about Money and Wealth
Re-Imagined and Updated for Today's Economy

Why You Should Read this Book

Do you worry about money? Having enough money to pay your bills? Figuring out how to pay for your student loans? Your rent? Your next meal?

Do you ever have the feeling that the financial system is overly complicated? Do you ever feel like the system is rigged? That it's working against you?

Guess what—you're right. The system is rigged. The modern American consumer-oriented economy is extraordinarily complicated. It thrives on service charges, fees, penalties, and interest. It is intensely data-driven, capable of identifying and targeting individuals precisely. It works efficiently and effectively—to separate you from your money.

Some people thrive in this kind of financial world. They may be the big beneficiaries of the system, getting paid so much that they don't have to worry about money. They may be the corporate executives who earn hundreds of times more than the average employee they supervise. Maybe they're investors who love to study financial data, industry trends, and they make money in the stock market. Maybe they're comfortable taking big risks. If the finances don't work out, it doesn't matter. Maybe they have a trust fund or something.

This book is for the rest of us.

Think about a worst-case scenario. No job. Lots of debt. And about the worst employment resumé you could possibly have. Most recent position? Inmate at Northern State Penitentiary.

How do you get on a path to financial security when that's where you're starting out?

The Richest Man in Babylon, a collection of pamphlets written in the 1920s by George S. Clason, tells stories about how to manage money. The stories are set in ancient Babylon. Characters with names like Bansir, Kobbi, Arkad and Algamish speak in an imaginary dialect, using phrases like "Fillith thy purse with gold." And yet, the book was very influential in its time and it is well-remembered even today.

This book, *The Richest Man in New Babylon,* builds on the principles contained in Clason's parables. It presents them for modern readers. It re-imagines and expands on these ideas in a new story set in a contemporary, mid-sized city somewhere in the United States. You will meet memorable characters who introduce a set of key principles for money management—the rules. You'll also learn to appreciate the additional personal and social skills required for success. And, as you follow one person's journey, the story offers one more vital element to help you along the path to financial security.

Hope.

This is a book for people who want to "keep it simple" when dealing with complex financial decisions. It's a book for people who want to cut through the clouds of consumerism and murk of marketing. It's a book for people who work hard and feel like they deserve to keep some of their hard-earned money.

The
RICHEST
MAN
in
NEW
BABYLON

An Inspirational Story about Money and Wealth
Re-Imagined and Updated for Today's Economy

RIDGE KENNEDY

HEDGEHOG HOUSE
WEST ORANGE, NEW JERSEY

Hedgehog House

28 Yale Terrace
West Orange, New Jersey 07052

973-400-9738 • www.hedgehoghousebooks.com

ISBN
Paper: 978-1-951989-02-6
E-Book: 978-1-951989-03-3

Publisher's Cataloging-in-Publication Data
Names: Kennedy, Ridge, author.
Title: The Richest Man in New Babylon / Ridge Kennedy.
Description: First Edition. West Orange, New Jersey
          Hedgehog House Books
Identifiers: LCCN: 2020910212 | ISBN 9781951989026
1. Personal Finance 2. Debt

Cover Design by Damonza.com
Jeanne Felfe, Editor — jeannefelfe@gmail.com
Michelle Krueger, Proofreader
Typeset by Affinity Publisher

10 9 8 7 6 5 4 3 2 1

Contents

Preface

In 2004, a flurry of interest in financial literacy at the New Jersey Society for Certified Public Accountants planted the seeds for this book. As a writer/public relations specialist at the Society, I got a call from someone looking for a speaker to address a group of women enrolled in a drug rehab program operated by Integrity House in Newark, NJ. It seemed like a great opportunity. We could ask one of our members, a personal finance expert, to volunteer to share important information with people facing major financial challenges.

With good intentions all around, a presentation was scheduled. A certified public accountant (CPA) with expertise in personal financial planning spoke for two hours. There might have been a PowerPoint presentation. There might have been a few useful handouts left for the attendees. I came away with a strong sense of what was *really* needed for this kind of program: more basics, more interaction with the students and more classroom time. No one-shot deals.

About a year later, I returned to Integrity House and began leading "The Money Class." The program managers at Integrity House asked me to work with male students who were still officially incarcerated in a halfway-house setting. Each class included a small group of eight to ten men. Typically, we met for six one-hour classes on consecutive Saturdays.

At first, the content of the classes was drawn from ideas suggested by the Integrity House staff; information I had gained from my writing assignments working with professional personal financial planners; books like *The Richest Man in Babylon;* and online research.

It was a learning experience for me. I learned about the financial challenges that the men faced. I learned that, in some ways, they knew a lot more about money than I did. I learned about approaches to leading the class that didn't work. And, through trial and error, I found two things that clicked—that seemed relevant and engaged the men. Stories: talking about people's experiences. And the rules.

After three years of leading the classes, I burned out. I felt that the organization wasn't supporting my efforts. I gave up. My bad. But I did not forget the experience and the lessons the men taught me. At some point—I'm not sure when—the idea of writing a story about a man and the rules occurred to me. I was familiar with the book—*The Richest Man in Babylon*—and its financial parables set in 5000 BC. I had interviewed personal financial planning professionals who recalled the book warmly. But, would those kinds of stories resonate with the men I had met? I didn't think so.

What about setting a story in the present day, in a contemporary American city? Call the city "New" Babylon?

In 2015, I started writing. Several drafts and several versions of the rules later, aided by the revolution in print-on-demand publishing, it is now available.

As I completed this "final, final" version of the book, I realized what it is: the book I wish I'd had when I was trying to lead The Money Class.

The Richest Man in New Babylon contains three primary elements.

First, there is a story—a "worst case scenario" for a general audience—but a realistic story that has been read and reviewed by men who have been incarcerated; a story that reflects the challenges they face. The language is G-rated so it's not authentic in that respect, but in most other ways, the story provides a true-to-life representation of real-world experiences.

Second: there are the rules. If a reader learns the rules and follows the rules, the reader will definitely benefit. I know this because I live by the rules myself. My wife and I have relied on them for decades and we have benefited by them.

Finally: there is hope. This is an optimistic story. A man in need meets a man—a good man—who introduces him to other people. He learns about networking, taking responsibility and earning peoples' trust. Out in the real world, many people in Jamaal's shoes will fail. Recidivism plagues the American correctional system. The support available for men like Jamaal is weak. This story, however, has a positive outcome.

This book does have limitations. There is important material that isn't addressed in the story. So, the book includes a closing "Afterwords" chapter where you will find additional information; things we might have discussed in the classes while we were continuing to reinforce the importance, relevance and simplicity of the rules.

The publication of *The Richest Man in New Babylon* is a not for profit enterprise. Books for use in correctional education and ex-offender reentry programs are made available at printing/shipping cost. Any profits from books sold to the general public will be used to expand access to the book through other media such as an audio book or Spanish translation.

Welcome to New Babylon, USA. The journey begins.

Ridge Kennedy,
West Orange, NJ
November, 2020

The Richest Man in New Babylon

Prologue

The first gunshot exploded by Jamaal's left ear.

A .357, Jamaal thought as he ducked and dropped to one knee on the sidewalk. Maybe a Glock 9. Damn loud anyway, even through the glass storefront. He couldn't hear anything on that side.

Jamaal scanned the street to his right. Any other shooters? If the first shot didn't get you, you probably weren't the target. Most dangerous thing now was crossfire. Being in the middle. Jamaal's companion—a big man—just stood there, staring in the convenience store window.

Three more shots from inside. Jamaal raised his head to look. A tall, skinny man was waving a handgun and—explosion—another shot. Shooting at cameras, Jamaal saw. Dumb. The cameras you see are all fake. Ain't gonna see the real cameras he thought, as he sank back down toward the sidewalk.

Jamaal scanned the street again, this time for cops. Not yet. But soon.

Another gunshot. Jamaal flinched. And—what the … ? Laughter? The big man standing next to him stared in the window—and laughed.

Jamaal wanted to run—away—anywhere. But he was frozen in place.

Running while black? With cops coming? Survival instinct kicked in. Stupid, he thought. Don't. Be. Stupid.

He took a deep breath. He remained still for a few more seconds, absorbing the chaos around him. Shouting and another gunshot in the store. More laughter. Was that a siren?

Jamaal caught a glimpse of his own reflection in the store window.

You …, he thought. You … stupid, stupid, stupid.

The Richest Man in New Babylon

Freedom

Jamaal stared out of the dirty window of the bus at two rings of chain-link fence topped with razor wire. The barriers, light poles, and guard towers surrounded a collection of gray cinder block buildings. For the first time in 368 days he was looking at the fences from the outside.

The Department of Corrections bus turned and rolled past the north side of the prison yard. It seemed to go on forever. Prison is big business in New Babylon. Mercy Hospital—that was the biggest employer in town. Then the government offices: city and county staff. Then the prison.

Jamaal looked at the bag on the empty seat next to him. One change of clothes, all too big. Sagging wasn't a fashion statement for him now; it was life. He felt in his pocket. One watch. Not running. One old cell phone. Dead. One wallet. No license. Just a prison ID. And forty-one dollars—mostly what he had the day of the sentencing. Plus, an envelope with six dollars in state pay.

The bus turned down an industrial highway now, passing brick factory buildings, mostly closed. A couple of warehouses showed signs of life. Junkyards were busy. The city impoundment lot.

Wheels, Jamaal thought. His wheels? Gone. Impound? Junkyard? Who knew? Didn't matter.

He tapped his pocket. Forty-one dollars, he thought. What the hell. Plus state pay—forty-seven bucks to his name.

The bus made its first stop at the railroad depot. You could still catch a train out of state, and there was a commuter line to take you to the airport. Buses there too, cheap buses, to get you out of town. That's what the city officials hoped for. Man gets out of incarceration—get that man out of town.

New Babylon was worn down and worn out. It had been a big city years ago—after the war. Good jobs. Nice place to live. But the factories closed. The jobs disappeared. They cut up the town with big highways and anyone with money moved to the suburbs.

Jamaal's bus stopped. End of the line. City Hall and the Justice Center on one side. Police Station across the street.

Jamaal stepped onto the sidewalk. And one convicted felon on the street, he thought.

He looked around. The uniforms that busted him. The suits who convicted him. It was like he still had his prison jumpsuit on. He had to get out of this place.

Jamaal's half-sister, Jennifer, she was going to give him a room. "For a few nights," she had said. "A few," she repeated. She would be home after work, maybe six o'clock.

Jamaal started walking. Across Broad Street, through that little alley, then away from downtown on Spruce or Pine or Maple or some other damn tree name.

He crossed MLK Boulevard. Now he now knew exactly where he was. Two blocks up High Street to Stewart Street. Roosevelt Middle School—three blocks to the right. The big AME church on the corner. All quiet right now. But come dark, the Doughboy and Pink and their crew, they'd be setting up shop.

Easy on—easy off from the highway. Suburban folk— they want to get in and get out. That's okay with the crew. Keep 'em moving. Good for business.

Come election time, the cops try to beat down on the trade. That was last year. It was stupid, Jamaal thought.

There weren't any jobs that summer. Not in fast food, not anywhere. And you could make more in one night than in a week at Mickey D's. Just pick up the merchandise. Take it to the customer. Bring back the cash.

Just his damn luck to get caught in an election year sweep. He took a customer's cash and outta nowhere—two damn cops. And he was going down. He was busted.

Jamaal kept walking up the hill, reliving the night, reliving the court proceedings. He had to accept the plea deal. If things went wrong, he'd have been looking at ten years. Maybe more.

Now he was looking back at a year of incarceration.

Could've been worse, he knew. He'd gotten a three-year bid. He got lucky, though. Overcrowding. Court order. They had to reduce the "population" so they let out some dumb kids like him to comply.

A year though. Long time.

He hadn't been beaten or raped or nothing. He was careful—didn't cross anyone. He survived. But it scared him. There's a bunch of scary dudes in prison—gangbangers, hotheads—don't care about nothing—shoot you as soon as look at you. And there are even scarier ones they keep on meds.

All of this raced through Jamaal's mind while he walked and walked and walked.

And then he stopped.

He was standing in front of a church in a small business district. Lots of little stores, all open, kind of busy. Clean sidewalks. Trees along the street. Hanging baskets on the light poles with flowers. Lots of flowers. Jamaal sat on a bench—one of two facing benches in front of the church. Some old dude—a short, very dark-skinned black man—was pushing a broom, sweeping the wide sidewalk in front of the church.

"Afternoon," the old man said.

"Afternoon," Jamaal said, nodding.

"You're new in our neighborhood," the old man said.

"Yeah," Jamaal said.

"Welcome," the old man said.

"Yeah," Jamaal said. "Yeah, I've been away for a while. Actually, I never been to this part of town."

"We're kind of tucked away," the old man said. "Not much changes around here. Lucky, I guess."

"What's it called," Jamaal said, "this place? Ain't the North Ward. Sure ain't the Homes or Orchard Street."

"Pacific Avenue, that's what we call the neighborhood," said the old man. He sat down on the bench across from Jamaal. "Name of this street. Not much to it, just a few blocks long. Goes a few blocks over on either side. Just a quiet little neighborhood."

"No gangs?" Jamaal said.

"Somehow we seem to have escaped their notice," the old man said. "Lots of people around here all the time, I guess there's easier places to hang out."

"Nice," Jamaal said. "I've been away for a while…"

"That's what you said."

"Any jobs around here?" Jamaal asked.

"Things come up," the old man said. "What's your name, son?"

"Who's asking?"

"Ah, introductions are in order," the old man said, standing up. "Ezekiel Wright, at your service."

He offered his hand. Jamaal didn't take it. The old man didn't look offended.

The old man sat down, this time on the bench next to Jamaal.

"'Course, almost nobody calls me by that name 'cept my Mama before she passed," the old man continued. "There's one fella, calls me Zeke, but most folks around here just call me Rev, on account of I pastored at this church for a few years."

"Rev, huh?" Jamaal said.

"Well, now it should be ex-Rev or Retired Rev or something, but Rev just seems to have stuck," the old man said. "They keep me on at the church, though—handyman, sweep steps, this and that."

"Yeah," Jamaal said.

"Yeah," the old man said. And then he didn't say anything for a while.

Jamaal looked over at the old man. Then looked straight ahead again.

"Yeah," Jamaal said. "Well ..."

Somewhere up the block a clock chimed five times.

"Well, gotta get moving," Jamaal said, standing up. The old man stood up next to him.

"Like I said, you hear about any jobs ..."

Jamaal looked at the old man—the Rev. He was short, mostly baldheaded, trim beard and mustache all going to white. He was short, but he wasn't small. Broad shoulders. Carried himself just so. One time, he was a strong man. Probably still punch way above his weight in his age group.

The old man—the Rev—wore thick glasses. Jamaal could see his eyes looking at him—looking through him just about. But not angry like. Not judging him. There was a smile. Lotta white teeth. Wrinkles in the corners of his eyes.

"I've been away for a while," Jamaal said.

"That's what you said."

"Jamaal. Jamaal Thomas," the younger man said, extending his hand.

"Pleased to meet you, Jamaal."

"Yes. Yes, sir. The same," Jamaal said. "Gotta get moving now."

Hanging with Old Friends

Jamaal left his half-sister's house at ten that night. Jennifer had stared through him with disapproval, but gave him a key and warned him not to tell anyone where he was staying.

"Doughboy," Jamaal said, dapping his former employer. Doughboy said he got his street name on account of he always had plenty of dough, but Jamaal had known him since grade school where his puffy body had earned him the nickname. He was a couple of inches shorter than Jamaal and outweighed him by a hundred pounds at least.

"Pink," Jamaal said, greeting Doughboy's taller, skinny companion with a dap and plenty of respect.

Pink had light brown skin and was as thin as Doughboy was fat. His hair, close cropped reddish blonde, had earned him his nickname. Pink had always been scary twitchy, which was good when you were an enforcer. Then Jamaal saw there was even more going on. In his fingers. In his eyes.

Pink's sampling the merch, Jamaal thought. He's using.

"Heard you was back," Doughboy said. "Damn if you ain't grown up some."

He was right. Jamaal had grown an inch taller and, with access to a weight room and nothing to do for a year, he was stronger. Strong and fit.

"You didn't have no trouble, did you? I told my boys inside to take good care of you," Doughboy said.

"No. No trouble," Jamaal said. Damn it, he thought. So that's why …

"Come on, man. Let's go to the Q-Mart. Grab some brew. Can't be away too long—business, you know. But we gotta celebrate—got you back."

They walked west on High Street toward the Q-Mart, Jamaal and Doughboy side-by-side and Pink trailing behind. Doughboy went on about "business," a truce he'd made with one gang, cop sweeps—there had been another, but it didn't last too long. Pink followed—then stopped, then hurried to catch up. Then stopped and started looking around.

Doughboy leaned closer to Jamaal and said, "My man Pink, getting a little nervous disorder, I think."

Jamaal nodded, and glanced at Pink as he walked past them, stumbled, caught himself and walked into the store.

"I might be looking for another full-time employee soon," Doughboy said. "We get you started part-time tonight. But there are growth opportunities."

Jamaal nodded, looking through the bars and window into the store. Doughboy stood back a ways, watching him.

There were about a dozen or twenty things he was hungry for. Frosted Flakes, he thought, seeing the cereal on a shelf. His daughter's favorite. Jameela and her mom, Natalie. He hadn't thought about them, not much except for all that child support. He sighed and thought about going into the store to buy a box.

That's when all hell broke loose.

Pink, standing in the middle of the candy aisle, had pulled out a gun and begun shooting. Ears ringing, Jamaal was hunkered down on one knee on the sidewalk outside.

Pink started shooting at surveillance cameras. Then he started waving his gun at the clerk. He was hollering. He wanted … cigarettes.

Pink screamed at the clerk, "Put the damn cigarettes in the damn bag."

Pink demanded cash now. The clerk was yelling in Arabic or something.

Doughboy started laughing. He just stood there, watching and laughing. He turned and started walking back down the street. Still laughing. And laughing.

Jamaal, still on one knee, stared back in the store window. Explosion. Pink put a bullet in the cash register.

Jamaal stood up and started walking—real slow—up the street—past the store, away from Doughboy.

Jamaal heard sirens now. Two, maybe three. Jamaal turned at the next corner and started to run. No, can't run, Jamaal thought to himself, slamming on the brakes. They see you running, they start shooting. He slowed down while his heart raced. Cop car, flashing lights—no siren— coming toward him, up the street.

Jamaal stopped at the corner. He waited as the cop car passed and then he crossed. Walking. Casually. His heart pounding. Damn, damn, damn, he thought.

Jamaal knew something now. Knew it through every atom of his body.

Jamaal Thomas did not want to go back to prison.

Looking for Pacific Avenue

Asking for directions—in the city he grew up in—that was embarrassing. Twice. Worse. But the next day, Jamaal found his way back to Pacific Avenue.

Early, he thought, just past nine. The old man wasn't there, in front of the church. Jamaal walked up to one end of the short street—only five blocks and back down the other. It was like he remembered: clean, no litter, no tags. Little stores, offices, a library, some kind of bank—a credit union—the sign said. Some places open, some still closed and a lot of folks all friendly like. He thought about buying coffee and maybe something more at a deli—then touched his wallet and decided "no." Too thin, he thought, my wallet is way too thin.

He started walking up and down the street again. He stopped in front of the small library at the far end of the street across from a little park. Still closed, but a friendly-looking place with lots of signs and posters about things going on and little kid pictures on the windows and stuff.

A bunch of children were crossing the street going the same direction. Must be a school that way, Jamaal thought. He looked down the cross street and saw signs and crossing guards a block away.

Parents were dropping off babies and tiny kids at a daycare center on the avenue. And there was just about every other kind of business, too. The library, the deli and the diner that he remembered, and a lot more: dry cleaners and a bakery, three or four more restaurants, two little food stores, doctors, lawyers, art and gift stores, and even a funeral home.

As he finished his third loop up and down Pacific Avenue, Jamaal saw the man he was looking for. He crossed the street.

"Old man," Jamaal said.

"Jamaal," the Rev said.

He was smiling. Now what did that mean? Jamaal thought. Disrespect?

"I was hoping I'd see you again," the old man said.

"Yeah," Jamaal started. "Yeah, well …"

It was about then that Jamaal realized he didn't have any idea what he wanted to say. He knew he wanted to talk to this old man. He wanted to say something—say everything—about last night—about tomorrow.

Jamaal just stood there, quiet, looking at the old man.

"How about a cup of coffee," the Rev said. "You drink coffee? Or tea, we got tea. Even got hot chocolate except that's out of an envelope and it ain't so good."

"Coffee," Jamaal said. "Yeah, coffee."

The old man pointed Jamaal around to the side of the church. They went up a short stairway, in through the side door, and down a small hall lined with offices, closets, a choir room, and such. They went into a little room at the end of the hall—a library sort of—with bookshelves all around and big comfortable chairs. The air already smelled of coffee. The old man went over to a little serving area built into the wall near the door.

"Always like to keep a pot warm, just in case," the Rev said. "Goes back to my pastoring days here. Cream? Real cream—no powder stuff. Sugar?"

"Just plain black," Jamaal said.

"The young folks now, they seem to like the tradition," he said, serving the coffee to Jamaal in a warm ceramic mug. "Or at least they like to humor me."

He sat down in a chair opposite Jamaal, cradling his own hot mug.

"So, how are you doing, Jamaal?" The old man looked at him with those kind old eyes. "I mean, how're you really doing? Yesterday, you said you just kind of stumbled into our little neighborhood. You pop up again today, I reckon this time, it must be on purpose."

Jamaal looked at the old man. Pause. Long pause.

"So, how you doing?" the Rev said.

"Well, you know, I've been away for a while …"

The old man nodded. "I know. I can see."

And Jamaal knew that the old man knew. And Jamaal started talking about what he'd done: incarceration, about his mom who struggled with drugs and now she was dead, and about knowing nothing about his dad. About his sister who made it and tried to help him but couldn't because he was a stupid kid, and more about incarceration and how he knew he'd been protected, and finally he talked about last night and how things had suddenly gone crazy, and how scared—how really scared he was—because he didn't want to be in the trade and have to worry every day about getting busted, and damn, damn, damn—he didn't want to go back to prison.

It was a half hour—maybe more—before he stopped talking.

He looked up at the old man—looked in his eyes.

"It's bad," Jamaal said.

The old man nodded.

"And it gets worse," Jamaal said. "It gets worse."

"I got no driver's license. Only identification I have is a prison ID card. I got no job. I got no money. Oh, but what I do have now, just to help me along, is a felony conviction. That means I can't get just about any job out there no matter how bad or low paying because ain't nobody gonna hire a convicted felon.

"Same time, to go along with all that good news, I do have fines on account of my conviction. I got some motor vehicle fines—speeding and a couple of red lights—and a bunch of parking tickets—and they charge interest and penalties on that. And when I got out of incarceration, they gave me a bill for 'supplementals.' Said I owed them $9.50 a day for them to keep me incarcerated.

"And on top of all of that, I got—I don't know how many thousands—in back child support.

"Let's ... let's add it all up," Jamaal continued. "Let's see where I stand. No job. No prospects except working for a drug dealer. No permanent place of residence. Thousands, maybe tens of thousands of dollars in debt and—oh yeah—forty-seven dollars in my wallet. The way I see it, I got nothing—nothing but trouble.

"What am I going to do?" Jamaal said, looking at the old man. "What the ... what the hell am I gonna do?"

Then he bent over and put his face in his hands.

"What am I gonna to do?" he said. Over and over. "What am I gonna do?"

Get Advice from a Rich Man

An hour later, Jamaal was pushing one of the old man's brooms out in front of the church. Three short strokes forward—then drop the broom head flat to shake out the dust and bits. Then back for a smooth cleanup stroke. Step to the side. Repeat. Move the line of debris forward.

"You gettin' the hang of that, now," the Rev said, admiring Jamaal's line of sweepings.

"Just copying the technique of a master," Jamaal said.

"I have decades of experience," the Rev said. "And from that wealth of experience, here's another tip."

Jamaal smiled and took a break from sweeping. He leaned on his broom.

"Wind direction," the Rev said. "Doesn't matter much today, but when you do feel some wind, you make sure to keep the wind at your back. Otherwise..."

"Sweep with the wind—it helps move stuff in the right direction," Jamaal said. "Go against the wind, it comes back at you."

"You catch on quick," the Rev said. "Same principle applies to peeing off the side of the ship."

"You have experience with that?" Jamaal laughed.

"I learned the hard way," the Rev said. "Things you learn the hard way—they seem to stick.

"Now, you are a tall, athletic man," the Rev said. "Play hoops?"

"Playground stuff," Jamaal said.

"Suppose you're on a team and you're pretty serious about it and you want to improve your shot. You want to be a great three-point shooter. What you gonna do?"

Jamaal looked at him and shrugged. "I don't know. Practice. Go out and shoot a lot of threes every day."

"Anything else?"

"Come on. What?" Jamaal said.

The old man didn't answer—just stood and waited.

"Okay," Jamaal said, breaking the silence. "How about I get a coach. Or at least find a guy who's good and watch him. Learn from him."

"Sure, you could do that. And ... ?"

"Ask for advice. Tips on how to shoot better."

"Coaching—good." The Rev continued, "And what if you decided you wanted to be a farmer and grow corn or apples or something?"

"That's a dumb idea, but if I was going to be a farmer, I'd want to talk to a farmer who grows lots and lots of corn or apples. Learn from an expert. Get coaching."

"Be a stamp collector?"

"Stamps? Like they stamp your hand at a party?"

"Postage stamps," the Rev said. "Put one on letter before you put the letter in the mail."

"They collect those things? Sounds really, really dumb," Jamaal said. "But—if I—for some crazy reason decided to collect postage stamps, I'd find me a real good postage stamp collector and ask for advice. See what he does. Get tips. Coaching."

"Sounds like a sensible plan," the Rev said. "So ...?"

"So? So?"

"You got a lot of bills and you ain't got a lot of money. So ...?

"Well, maybe ... maybe I can find some rich man and get coaching, and tips and learn all the secrets about how to get rich," Jamaal said.

"Well, someone with some money," the Rev said.

"You started this so, let's go all in," Jamaal said. "I want to meet the richest man in New Babylon."

"Well ..."

"So, old man, can you deliver on that? Introduce me to the richest man in New Babylon?" Jamaal asked.

The Rev looked at Jamaal carefully and, after a pause said, "I believe I can."

"Okay."

"But first, there are a few things you have to do," the Rev said. "Some preliminaries. You ready for that? This money stuff—it's like a game. You're going to have to learn the rules."

In War, You Need People on Your Side

"This is the young man?"

Jamaal faced a big, dark-skinned man—bigger than the Rev. The man's close-cropped hair, going to gray, had given up trying to cover the top of his head. Not quite as tall as Jamaal—but wider. He filled the doorway.

"Take it easy on him, Gunny," the Rev said.

"Easy?" Gunny said.

"Just to get started," the Rev said.

"Come in," Gunny said. "Welcome. Let's set up shop in the dining room."

Gunny lived in a small house, all wood, painted different colors with lots of decorations on it. Trees out front shaded the lawn and flower beds that were—well—perfect. The inside the house was both comfortable and neat—everything straight and orderly and not a bit of clutter.

Right at the front door, there was a small hallway with a closet and a large, high-backed antique bench that had a big mirror and lots of hooks for hanging hats and coats.

Straight ahead, Jamaal saw a comfortable-looking living room. Gunny led them off to the right and into a bright, sunlit dining room. The big table had eight chairs around it. Gunny sat at the head and invited Jamaal to sit on his right. The Rev, clearly at home, went into the kitchen. A pot of coffee, mugs, milk, and sugar were already on the table.

"Help yourself," Gunny said, gesturing toward the coffee.

Jamaal picked out a mug and poured.

"Zeke tells me you've got some money problems."

"Zeke?" Jamaal said.

"Ezekiel. The Rev. That old man currently ransacking my kitchen looking for … what are you looking for in there, Zeke?"

"Some kind of little snack. A bite of something," the Rev said from the kitchen.

"There's some of them funny little carrots in the produce drawer of the fridge," Gunny said. "And a bag of them gingersnap cookies you like on top the fridge.

"Now, we were talking money," Gunny said, turning toward Jamaal.

"More like no money," Jamaal said. "No money and everybody in the world wants to get paid."

"And you're thinking … ?" Gunny said. "Zeke said something about talking to a very wealthy man? Find someone who's rich and … ?"

"Well, I was just talking with the Rev about this and that," Jamaal said. "He's the one who said he could do it—help me meet the richest man in New Babylon. Get advice. Get some tips. Learn how to get me some real money."

The Rev came back in the dining room with a small plate full of gingersnap cookies.

"If either of you gentlemen really want some of them carrots, you just tell me and I'll go fetch some for you," he said. "Well, Jamaal, now you've met the Gunny," the Rev said.

"The richest man?" Jamaal said. "You mean, he's …"

"Not quite," Gunny said, laughing. It was a good laugh. Comfortable.

"You know about someone bein' a Gunny?" the Rev asked Jamaal.

Jamaal shrugged. "Funny name," he said.

"Gunny ain't a name so much as it's a title," the Rev said. "Jamaal, you are talking to Gunnery Sergeant Malcolm T. Forrester, United States Marine Corps, Retired. Gunny, meet Jamaal Thomas—a smart young man from what I can tell. Had some troubles in the past, looking to dig himself out of a pretty deep hole."

Marine Corps, Jamaal thought looking at the man next to him. Yeah, Marine Corps.

"I met Gunny about a hundred years ago when I was serving," the Rev was saying. He was just a staff sergeant then, but he was already pretty good at kicking butt and taking names. He got me off to a damn good start in the Corps.

"I didn't stay in, but we've kept up all these years. I reckon any young man looking for a good place to start can't go wrong with right here, with the Gunny."

"Hey, I appreciate what you're saying," Jamaal said. "But just so's you know, I ain't planning on going to war—join the Corps or anything like that."

Gunny smiled. "Good thing, too, Jamaal," he said. "Because they won't have you. Man with any kind of police record—it's very difficult to get in the service today."

"Oh," Jamaal said. "Yeah. I should have …"

"But," Gunny continued, "let me correct you on one other point." He paused.

Jamaal waited. "Go on," he said finally.

"You *are* going to war, son," Gunny said. "You got enemies out there," he said making a broad gesture toward the windows. "You got enemies in here," he said putting his fist against his chest.

"You got battles to fight," Gunny said, leaning closer to Jamaal and seizing him with his eyes. "You're going to win some—you can even hope—win most of these battles," he went on. "But you are going to lose some, too. And you are going to have to keep fighting. Keep going. And you know why are you going to have to keep going?"

Jamaal didn't say anything.

"Because it's a damn war," Gunny said, "and you got a hell of a lot to learn if you want to win it."

"You got to know who your friends and allies are—who you can trust—who's on your side.

"Even more important—you got to know your enemy—your enemies—because when it comes to money in this modern world—you have enemies everywhere.

"You got to have a battle plan." Gunny was really rolling now. "It's going to change, but at least you'll understand your position better. Develop a strategy. Make good decisions.

"You gotta have strength—physical and mental. You gotta have training—learn to use information and all the tools at your disposal. They are your weapons.

"You're going to need discipline. The road is going to be rough. It's gonna suck. It's gonna beat you up and get you down. But you gotta keep going!

"If all that sounds pretty damn bad—well it is. You're in a bad place and you're going to have to fight a hell of a damn war to get out of it.

"I'm laying out all the bad stuff—the tough stuff—so's you understand that what you want to do—it is not easy. But—listen to me good here—it is not impossible either.

"You are smart. You are strong. You are young—you have lots and lots of time.

"There's one more thing that's essential for a man who's going to war. You gotta have good morale. You gotta believe in your mission and keep after it. And from time to time you need a little R&R—rest and recreation. You need buddies, people you can trust, to help keep you going.

"The Rev here, he'll tell you that you got to take care of your spiritual self, too. Gettin' churched—real church—ain't such a bad thing.

"In the service, I got to know all kinds of Christians and Jews and Buddhists and Muslims. I got to where I kinda believe in everything. I can just sit on the front porch quiet like a Quaker and just try to feel the world pass by—hear all the sounds and feel the air and—it just makes me feel good inside. So, there's another thing for your battle plan—to take care of your spiritual self."

Gunny stopped talking, sat back and took a sip of coffee.

Jamaal sat. It was a long time before he spoke.

"When do I start," Jamaal finally said.

Gunny glanced over at the Rev and then back at Jamaal.

"This is a serious undertaking—this war you're going to have to fight. I think I gave you a whole lot to think about," Gunny said.

Jamaal laughed. Not because it was funny.

"You think about everything I've been saying," Gunny said. "If you're ready to go to war—you come back here—same time tomorrow—and we'll get started.

"Like I said—it's going to be hard. Damn hard. You gotta be ready to work hard, and hurt and sacrifice. If you're not ready for that—don't come back.

"But if you do come back, the Rev and me, we're going to be here," Gunny said. "We're gonna be your buddies. We're going to be ready to go to war with you."

The Richest Man in New Babylon

Rule Number 1

Jamaal rang the doorbell precisely at ten o'clock the next morning. Gunny opened the door. Back in the now familiar dining room, the Rev was waiting. After coffee was poured, they were all seated.

"You're ready?" Gunny said, inspecting Jamaal's face intently. Jamaal didn't look away.

"Thought about everything you said. Thought about it hard," Jamaal said. "I'm ready."

"Here," the Rev said, pushing a black-and-white school composition book and pen toward Jamaal. "You better start writing this stuff down. Top of the page—put this down. 'The Rules.' Then you can add 'em there as you learn 'em."

"The Rules," Jamaal said, taking pen in hand in writing on the first page of the composition book.

"Rule number one," Gunny said. He paused. "Pay yourself first."

"Pay yourself first," Jamaal said, writing.

"Now, tell me what you think that means," Gunny said.

"It's about, I guess, paying for your own stuff first," Jamaal said. "Before you start treating other folks?"

"Not even close," Gunny said. "But you're new to this kind of thinking. We'll take it step-by-step.

"Working for a living—no matter what you do—usually it's—well, it's work," Gunny said. "You on board with that?"

"Sure," Jamaal said.

"Let's say you're in construction. Spend long days working in the hot sun. End of the week, man gives you a check—a couple hundred bucks and change," Gunny said. "Now what?"

"Pay for stuff," Jamaal said. "Gotta pay rent and buy food. And … come on Gunny, you know I got a ton of stuff I got to pay for now—all the fines and child support and stuff."

"Let's think about that," Gunny said. "You worked hard, right? Damn hard. Don't you think you deserve to *keep* some of that money?"

"Well, sure. I'd like to," Jamaal said. "But like I said— rent, food, other stuff—there ain't going to be much left."

"Chances are there won't be anything left," Gunny said. "Hell, with you just gettin' started, it's one hundred percent certain there won't be anything left.

"And you may not waste a penny. You'll just pay for things that are really important—and in the end—you'll be broke."

"Yeah, I guess," Jamaal said. "When you're in a hole, that's how it is."

"Doesn't have to be," Gunny said. "Rule number one: Pay yourself first. The first, most important bill you pay every time you get even a little bit of money—you save some of it. You pay *yourself* first."

"But," Jamaal said. "I got all these bills and expenses and stuff …"

"You already said you won't be able to pay them all," Gunny said. "You're going to pay some and put off others. And when that money is gone, you're still gonna have stuff to pay for—right?"

"Yeah, that's right," Jamaal said

"Okay. What's the difference?" Gunny said. "Ignore rule number one. Money runs out. You are broke and in debt."

"Yeah," Jamaal said.

"Pay yourself first," Gunny continued. "Money runs out and you're still in debt. But you are not broke. You got savings. Maybe just a little to start. But you got something. You are *not* broke."

"Yeah, but …" Jamaal said.

"You pay yourself first and you start taking control of things," Gunny said. "You decide for yourself. You're not just letting bills and debts determine everything you do with your money.

"You want to be broke?" Gunny asked.

"No," Jamaal said.

"How can you be sure you won't be broke?"

There was a pause. Gunny waited.

"Pay yourself first?" Jamaal said.

"You aren't really believing it yet. But you're getting the idea."

"When you got so little money to start with, it's hard," Jamaal said.

"That's why the rule is so important," Gunny said. "You put off saving, you're never gonna get around to it. All the other stuff gets in the way."

"Pay yourself first," Jamaal said. He paused. "I mean, it sounds good," he continued. "But what if it's not much? Why would it matter?"

"Three things," Gunny said. "First, anything is a whole lot when you compare it to nothing. You either got money or you're broke. That's a big deal.

"Second point—you put time on your side. You know how a leaky pipe can work—one little drip at a time—slow like. Let it go—next thing you got water all over the floor. Fill up the whole damn basement like a swimming pool. But it's just this little bitty drip, you were thinking.

"Saving works the same way. Little bit at a time—drop by drop—but it adds up.

"And it matters because it puts *you* in control. When you have savings, you can make your own decisions.

"You got some old debt hanging over your head. You got enough money saved—maybe you decide to get rid of that debt. Bang, pay it off. You're in control."

"Pay yourself first," Jamaal said. Then he repeated it. "Pay yourself first."

"And it means?" Gunny said, looking hard at Jamaal.

"Treat your savings like a bill—the first and most important bill you have to pay," Jamaal said

"I think he's got it," the Rev said.

"Could not have stated it any better myself," Gunny said.

THE RULES
1. PAY YOURSELF FIRST

Paying Your Way

"That's the end of our 'rules' for today," Gunny said. Jamaal sat back in his chair and relaxed a little.

"So, how are you doing?" the Rev asked. "Where are you staying? Got any work lined up?"

"Staying with my sister," Jamaal said. "Half-sister. She said I could stay a few days."

"It's been a few days since I met you," the Rev said.

"Yeah," Jamaal said. "Yeah."

"Got a backup plan?" the Rev asked.

"Not really," Jamaal said.

"Maybe you can pay some rent to your sister," Gunny said. "Might make her more inclined to keep you on a little longer."

"I've only got—like thirty dollars and some change," Jamaal said.

"You eating any of her food?" Gunny asked.

Jamaal nodded.

"She's putting a roof over your sorry head," Gunny continued.

They sat in silence for a while.

"Job prospects?" the Rev said.

"Nothing," Jamaal said. "Any place hiring, they got 'have you ever been convicted' on the application. You tell the truth, ain't no way they gonna hire you."

After a pause he went on. "Only place hires people like me around here is the packing house. Worst damn work anywhere. Freezing cold, wet, bloody, and damn dangerous, too. Guys lose fingers every day, get cut up bad."

"They hiring?" Gunny said.

"They always hiring, least that's what I heard, back when …"

"So that's a possibility?" the Rev said.

"Yeah," Jamaal said. "It's a possibility."

"Something to do while you get things together," the Rev said. "An' meanwhile, to help you get started looking further, there's the library—just up the block from here. They got a lot of job resources. Help you get yourself on-line with a resumé and all the stuff you need these days. First job you take doesn't have to be the last," the Rev said. "You do know that?"

Jamaal nodded. He finished his cup of coffee. He looked back and forth between the two men.

"Oh, just so you know, you gonna have more like twenty five dollars," Gunny said.

"How's that?" Jamaal said.

"Going to cost you five dollars minimum, to join our credit union," Gunny said. "Right up the street. Open right now."

Jamaal felt his shoulders tighten and clenched his right fist. These old men, telling him what to do with his money. Damn. He looked at the Rev, then at Gunny, then back at the Rev. The anger passed. Jamaal sighed. He nodded.

"Pay yourself first," he said.

Both of the older men broke out smiles and nodded.

The Difference Between Broke and Not Broke

Jamaal arrived at his sister's house tired. Bone weary tired. After the stop at the Pacific Avenue Credit Union, he'd walked miles. Miles and miles. But he found out that, yes, they were hiring at the packing house. But he needed steel-toed safety shoes, and the Salvation Army Thrift Shop on the other side of town might have some.

After his hike, he found out they didn't, but Goodwill Industries might and that wasn't too far away. Jamaal got lucky. Goodwill was still open. Even though he got there right at five, they let him in. And they had some shoes—a little too big, but they would do.

Another long walk and he met his sister as she was getting home from work.

"Jennifer," he said, as they got into the front hallway. Jamaal took out his wallet and took all the remaining bills out—a one, a five, and a ten.

"Thank you for putting me up here for a while," Jamaal said. "Here," he said, giving her the money. "Ain't enough, but I want to help with the expenses, you know."

"Good," she said. "That's good," she said as she took the money.

She paused. She looked at Jamaal and he met her eyes.

"You're looking a little different," she said.

"Had a lot of time to work out," he said.

"No, not that. Just, maybe a little older. More grown up." She smiled, just a bit.

"Good," she said again, putting the expense money in a front pocket. She nodded and went into the kitchen.

Jamaal put his empty wallet away.

Broke, he thought, except for a little loose change.

Then he thought about the old-fashioned savings passbook he had in his shirt pocket and managed a slight smile.

No, not broke, he thought. Just a little short on cash at the moment.

Looking for Work—Get Online or Give Up

Parker. Damn Arvin Parker, Jamaal thought. If there was one thing Jamaal would do—he would find a job where he didn't have to work for Arvin Parker, the biggest pain in the rear end that Jamaal had ever met, and that included a whole lot of teachers and social workers, and even prison guards.

Parker was dark-skinned, a little shorter than Jamaal, but wiry and strong. He could have been forty or sixty—

hard to tell with his shiny bald head. Jamaal didn't like the man, and he didn't want to mess with him either.

Parker supervised the day shift at the packing house and he was all over everyone about stuff. But it seemed like he always had something extra for Jamaal.

Gotta be something better I can do, Jamaal thought. He was motivated. He'd do anything to get away from that jumped up, trash talking, sorry old man.

Jamaal stood in line at the reference desk in the Pacific Avenue Branch Library. Two little kids were in front of him, asking about books. Jamaal looked around.

The place was crawling with kids. Jamaal got off work at four and by the time he got to the library, every computer was in use and kids were sitting around all the reading tables, too. It was noisy for a library, Jamaal thought. A kind of a busy, happy place, he was thinking, but not real quiet.

"Can I help you?" the librarian asked.

Jamaal jumped back from his daydream.

"Sorry," he said. "Need to use a computer. Got some work to do—getting a job and such."

"May I see your library card," the librarian said.

"Ahh, I don't have one," Jamaal said. "How much does one cost?"

The librarian—Mrs. Ross, it said on her name badge—looked a little surprised and smiled at Jamaal.

"There's no charge. This is a public library," Mrs. Ross said. "No charge for your library card and no charge for using the computers.

"You will, however, have to pay if you need to print things out. That's ten cents a page.

"Marie," she said to another woman sitting at a desk behind the counter, "can you step in here for a minute. I need to assist a new patron who needs a library card."

For the next twenty minutes, Mrs. Ross, this nice, kind of middle-aged white lady, helped Jamaal get ready to rid himself of Arvin Parker.

First a library card—just a piece of plastic like a credit card with a bar code on it. He used his sister's house as his address.

"You don't live very far from our main branch," Mrs. Ross said.

"Sure," Jamaal said. "I know where it is. But I'm spending some time over on this side of town. I kinda like the neighborhood."

"So do we," Mrs. Ross said, smiling. "So do we."

"Now," she continued, "let me take you on a tour of our Employment Resource Center. We have books and on-line resources for resumé preparation, career guides, employment databases, and, of course, access to all the websites with job listings. We've also got links to the State Workforce Development Center and …"

Mrs. Ross went on for about ten or fifteen minutes, talking about building an online presence and career resources and visiting job boards and more. She was trying to be helpful, but even with the handout sheets and brochures she gave him, Jamaal was having a hard time taking it all in.

Mrs. Ross was talking about another kind of online database, and then she stopped and looked at Jamaal.

She smiled.

"Too much information," she said, mostly to herself. "Sorry," she said, now speaking to Jamaal. "I helped plan and put together our Employment Resource Center. I get a little carried away sometimes.

"We have some great resources here for you. And we're here to help you get started using them.

"First things first, let's get you online," she said.

Then Mrs. Ross showed Jamaal how to sign up for computer time. She took him to a computer in a study room that wasn't in use and went through the login procedure. Jamaal hadn't had much experience with computers in high school—the schools didn't have many and they were mostly old and slow, if they worked at all. And after he left school—well, working for Doughboy—not much call for developing your computer skills there. While he was incarcerated Jamaal signed up for computer classes, but he never got in them. Outside of those classes, any computer stuff had to go through JPay*. What a rip. Music? Messages? Money? Yeah, sure. But it costs you.

After Jamaal logged into the library computer, he sat and stared at the screen for a minute. He sighed, turned and saw Mrs. Ross still hovering fairly close by. He caught her eye and she came over.

"I'm sorry," he said. "I never had much experience with computers—played some games when I was little, but most of the serious stuff … I don't know very much at all. Would you mind helping me get started?"

Mrs. Ross sat down next to him. She slowed down her flow of information and showed him how to use the web browser. She helped him create an e-mail account. She explained how important your login name and password were, and told him about some bad things that can happen if you get "hacked."

When Jamaal left the library at six, he was a little dazed. But he had a library card and an e-mail address. He knew there was a lot more stuff associated with the e-mail address, too. He had a "cloud" for storing things, and programs for writing up resumés and letters. And one very cool thing Mrs. Ross explained to him, he could get to all his stuff from any computer anywhere, as long as it was connected to the Internet. Even better—all of it was free.

And he was signed up for a computer class at the library, too. It was mostly for older people who hadn't used computers much or at all, Mrs. Ross told him.

"I may not have any gray hair, but the rest, that sounds like me," Jamaal said. "Sign me up."

---

*Editor's note: JPay is a for-profit company that works, under contract, with many corrections systems, to provide money transfers, banking/credit services, communications, entertainment and other services. The company pays "commissions" to corrections systems. Critics describe many of its services and practices as overpriced, unfair and/or predatory. It is one of many for-profit businesses operating in the corrections industry.

The Richest Man in New Babylon

Rule Number 2

Jamaal met the Rev in front of the church on Pacific Avenue a little before noon on Sunday. The old man was suited up—a brown, three-piece ensemble, and he was wearing a narrow-brimmed fedora. Somehow, the dapper image he cut amused Jamaal.

"Dude," Jamaal said, greeting the old man warmly. "Get yourself a walking stick man. You're ready to step out in some kind of movie."

Jamaal's clothing still hung on him—giving him a scarecrow look. He could do laundry at his sister's house—a blessing. At the end of next week, he'd be getting his first paycheck from the packing company.

"You said we were on for something today," Jamaal said. "Talking money. You gonna introduce me to the richest man today? Gunny on board?"

"Yes, no and yes, but not physically present—the Gunny that is," the Rev said. He pointed, and he and Jamaal began walking up the street.

"Recap for me," the Rev said, as they crossed the street to the other side of Pacific Avenue. "Rule number one."

"Pay yourself first," Jamaal said.

"Explain," the Rev said.

"Treat your savings like it's the first, most important bill you have to pay," Jamaal said.

"Okay," the Rev said. "You got the words down. It'll take some time now. See how you do with it."

"Hey, I've done the deed," Jamaal said, patting the passbook in his shirt pocket. "I'm a rich man now," he said. "Doubled down on the minimum. Ten whole dollars," he said, shaking his head. Then, more seriously, he said, "You report that back to Gunny."

The Rev paused about halfway up the third block from the church, went through a door between two stores and into a small hallway at the foot of a long flight of stairs. He pressed a button below one of the two mailboxes. The name on the mailbox said Chen Lee Mae.

They were met at the top of the stairs by a small, Asian woman who ushered them into—well—not a room—a space—one big open space.

"Welcome," she said with a slight accent. "Welcome to my studio."

"Chen Lee Mae," the Rev said, "this is the young man I spoke to you about. Jamaal Thomas. Jamaal, allow me to introduce you to Chen Lee Mae, my favorite artist in residence here on Pacific Avenue."

"Pleased to meet you, Miss Mae," Jamaal said.

"Oh," the Rev said, "Chinese names. First name last and last name first. So, it's Ms. Chen who'll be our instructor for the day."

"Mae," the petite woman in blue jeans, white shirt, and sandals said. "Please, just call me Mae. Would you like me to show you around my studio?"

Jamaal nodded, and Mae led them around the enormous room. Part of the space was dedicated to painting. Three big easels with canvases in varying stages of completion on them, stood near the front windows. A large printing press took up space along one wall. The center of the room looked like an art gallery with paintings and prints hung on movable walls and interesting looking sculptures on pedestals. A kitchen occupied the back of the large, open space. The stove, a fridge and lots of cabinets lined most of the back wall. The bedroom, a sleeping loft reached by a ladder, formed a "second story" above the kitchen area. A small bathroom with a shower took up the corner opposite the studio's front door.

Mae motioned the men to a small round table near the stove. The dining room, Jamaal thought.

"Tea?" Mae asked.

The Rev nodded. Jamaal followed the old man's example and nodded, too. Mae took a hot kettle off the stove. She took loose tea, filled a small metal ball with it and put it in a teapot. She poured the hot water then and allowed the tea to steep while they discussed the weather, the growing number of artists moving to Pacific Avenue, a new gallery for the art co-op, and Mae's plans for a trip to New York to see her sister and to speak with some gallery representatives. Tea was poured. Finally, they were all seated around the table, each with a hot cup.

"Jamaal is facing some severe financial challenges, Mae. He's working now, but the pay isn't great. He's worried," the Rev began.

Mae smiled. "When you are an artist," she said, "especially when you are a young artist, you learn a lot about not having much money. That is why Reverend Wright wanted me to share my experience with you."

Jamaal nodded.

"I can sum this all up in one sentence," she said.

"Your notebook, Jamaal," the Rev said. "You can write this down. Rule number two."

"Oh, rule number two is it?" Mae said, laughing. "I am honored to rank so highly on your list."

"Then—rule number two," she continued. "If you want to have more money, spend less."

Jamaal repeated the words as he wrote them down in his notebook. "If you want to have more money, spend less."

When he finished writing, Jamaal looked up at Mae and the Rev.

"Easy for you to say," Jamaal said.

"Not easy all the time. Sometimes quite challenging," Mae said. "But you may also find that not spending money can be fun, exciting, liberating. It can spur your imagination and draw on your creativity."

"You make it sound like being broke is a blessing," Jamaal said.

"You're broke?" the Rev said.

Jamaal smiled. "Being short on cash," he said.

"Look around you," Mae said. "Not the art. Everything else. Maybe it's easier for a young artist. You are full of passion for your own work. You know you won't have lots of money so you improvise and use your creativity.

"Look around," she repeated. "Nearly everything you see here except the artwork, I found somewhere on the street or near a dumpster.

"Even the art for that matter—I use many things that other people have discarded.

"It's a matter of having a special kind of eyesight—seeing something unique or useful where someone else sees something to be thrown away."

"Look, I understand, stuff like tables and chairs," Jamaal said. "But what about personal stuff? Shoes? Clothing? Man's got to dress, you know."

"Glad you brought that up," the Rev said. "You are looking a little raggedy. Now how do you like this suit I'm wearing?"

"Nice. Nice threads," Jamaal said.

"Big-name designer fashion," the Rev said. "Cost me ten dollars at the thrift store."

"Damn," Jamaal said. "Looks custom."

"It didn't fit exactly right when I got it. But I took it to our tailor—Mr. Roman—just up the block. I put another twenty dollars into it. But still—a fine suit that fits perfectly for thirty dollars," the Rev said.

"What about stuff like a cell phone plan and cable TV?"

"I have a mobile telephone," Mae said. "It sends and receives e-mail and text messages. It meets all my needs and costs a little more than one hundred dollars per year. All quite reasonably priced."

"Cable TV?" the Rev said. "You think you *need* cable TV?

"Let me tell you about one of the best-kept secrets of life in these modern times," the Rev said. "It's called an antenna. Comes in all shapes and sizes—attach it to your TV and bingo—the best TV picture you can get."

"Yeah, but for movies and stuff …?"

"That's what you got your library card for," the Rev said.

"A lot of sports I want to see," Jamaal said.

"If it's worth watching and it isn't on free TV, find a buddy or stop in the Senior Center," the Rev said.

"Sometimes you must spend your money," Mae said. "When your physical health is a concern, you must see a physician for a checkup. If you require an essential medication, yes you must buy and take it."

"You can't totally deprive yourself either—try to live like some saint," the Rev said. "That's why you set aside a little cash—a little walking around money—and say you're gonna spend it on anything you damn well please. Just blow it.

"But," the Rev added, "you only spend that cash you *plan* to blow. You never spend any more than that."

"That is an interesting thought," Mae said. "I never planned to spend money without a plan."

"I suspect that this is a guy thing," the Rev said. "Something men do more than women?"

"Oh, women can spend quite impulsively too," Mae said.

"Well, here's my thing," Jamaal said, jumping into the conversation. "I want to have more money but I'm not a cheapskate. Man wants respect—got to flash some cash."

"Seriously, Jamaal," the Rev said. "Who are you going to respect more—a man who spends his last few dollars on something he doesn't need or a man with cash in his wallet and money in the bank?"

"I need ..." Jamaal started.

"Need," the Rev cut him off. "That's the key word."

"How do you know if you really *need* something instead of it being something you just *want?*"

"What are the consequences if you *do not* spend the money?" Mae said. "What is the worst possible thing that can happen?"

"Will someone die?" the Rev continued. "Will someone be ill or be seriously injured? Will someone be arrested? Will you cause yourself a financial setback just when you're starting to move forward?"

"If you want to have more money, spend less," Mae said. "What is more important? Having more money or having to worry about what some other people think about you?"

"You listen to her," the Rev said. "I see you're nodding your head, but I know how you young people can be, wanting some special kind of this or fancy bit of that.

"No artist with think badly of you," Mae said. "Maybe you should just declare yourself to be 'struggling artist.' Then, no problem."

Jamaal laughed—at the way she said it and at the idea that he could ever be an artist. He didn't even mind how they had ganged up on him.

"Okay," he said. "Okay. I get it. If I want to have more money, spend less. I'm not spending hardly anything now, but I understand what you're saying."

THE RULES

1. PAY YOURSELF FIRST

2. IF YOU WANT TO HAVE MORE MONEY—
   SPEND LESS

The Richest Man in New Babylon

Sorry, Company Policy

P arker was on his case again. The Spanish guys on the line—he wasn't sure where they all came from—they just all spoke Spanish and hardly any English—and they always seemed to get more done than Jamaal. While he was trimming up three big cuts, they would do four. Jamaal took fifteen-minute breaks every two hours, like the company said you could. The Hispanics—they worked right on through to lunch or the end of the shift.

And Parker, always on his back, found special jobs for Jamaal since he was so bad at cutting and trimming. That's how Jamaal got assigned to do cleanup—clearing the work areas and scraping stuff up off the floor. He hauled buckets of leavings around and dumped them for processing into pet food or worse. And he got completely soaked with bleach water while sanitizing work tables and processing equipment.

And it seemed like wherever he was, Arvin Parker was right behind him, sayin', "you missed this," and "it'd be more efficient if you did it this way," and finding more work for him to do the instant he finished something up.

Jamaal was being systematic about his job search. He only applied to places he could get to without a car. He was being realistic about his qualifications—he wasn't a computer programmer. He was looking for warehouse work, laborer jobs, maintenance—clean and push a broom jobs. It was all stuff he knew he could do.

Some places he applied in person. For others, he applied online. Some places you went in to apply and they sat you down at a computer and you applied online.

The people he met seemed nice, and some, he could tell right away, he could get along with them. Every time he finished up a new application, he was feeling almost hopeful.

Except for that one thing. That question.

Have you ever been convicted of a felony?

Yes.

No.

If you answered 'yes', please explain.

Every application had that question or something an awful lot like that question.

He started out saying "yes" and then wrote out his "explanation."

"I was young and just finished high school, and I didn't have a job," he would write. "Someone I knew offered me some work. I made a terrible mistake. The work was not legal, and I was arrested. I have been working very hard to make up for my mistake. Please give a young man who's made a mistake an opportunity to do better."

Mostly, he never heard anything back. Once in a while, he'd get a letter from a place saying they had filled the position he applied for, but they would keep his resumé on file.

Jamaal had looked it up online, whether job applications could ask about your criminal background. The information he found was confusing. Some states said you could ask. Some said you couldn't. Federal law seemed to suggest you should not ask the question about felonies because so many African American men had convictions, it would be racial discrimination.

Sure, it seemed like companies were not supposed to ask about convictions, but a lot of them did anyway.

Jamaal decided to stop answering the question: just ignore it. It didn't make any difference.

Finally, he started checking "no." No convictions.

He got a job interview for a warehouse. It went really well. They made a job offer, and he accepted—he'd be starting in two weeks.

Two days after the interview, he got another phone call on his sister's answering machine. There was a problem.

Jamaal called and talked to the woman in human resources he had met. She said the company had checked his credit report—part of their standard procedures for hiring new people—and there were some problems. It wasn't clear where he had been living for the last year or so.

Jamaal tried to explain. He'd been young. He got in some trouble. And well … he … he'd been incarcerated.

The woman on the phone was nice enough, but just said he had "misrepresented" himself in his application.

"That wouldn't be a good way to start an employment relationship," she said. And she pulled the job offer.

Meanwhile, Arvin Parker had Jamaal coming in early to do more disinfecting work. Then he'd keep him late, to take care of cleanup work during the shift change. And it never satisfied Parker, who was always looking to find fault.

Jamaal just knew he had to get out of that place.

A Different Kind of Work

The Big AME church on High Street was looking for a janitor. They posted the job on the Workforce Development bulletin board.

Jamaal had learned how to keep track of the listings and tried to pounce on anything that looked possible as soon as it appeared. But this listing was three days old.

The notice said "apply in person." Jamaal printed out a copy of his resumé, logged off the library computer, went to the reference desk to pay for his copies, and hurried off toward the church. This was a well-worn path for him—it would take twenty minutes. He would be there before five and get the application in today.

Except the church office wasn't open. Jamaal stayed a few minutes, hoping someone would show up. He thought about slipping his resumé under the door or leaving it in the mailbox—and figured that would just be a waste. But he left it in the mailbox anyway.

He walked back up the path along the side of the church to High Street, and as he stepped on the sidewalk, he nearly ran into Doughboy.

The big man reacted, flinched and turned—then recognized Jamaal.

"Ahh, it's you. Jamaal. My man." Now he sounded all friendly-like. "Haven't seen you in weeks. Where you been hiding?"

"Just working," Jamaal said. "Working hard. No time to be running around."

"What kind of work?" Doughboy asked.

"Crummy work," Jamaal replied honestly, thinking about Parker and his demands. "Down at the packing plant."

"Oh," Doughboy said. "Now I've heard stories about that place. Cold all the time, damn near freezing. Wet and nasty. Lotta guys get cuts. You been cut up at all?"

Jamaal clenched his hands and ran his thumbs over his fingers. He thought he could still feel the chill in them from his work today.

"Nah," Jamaal said, answering Doughboy's question. "When I do cuttin' work, I've got safety gloves. Knife can't cut through them, even if you try. I'm doing more maintenance work now, not so much cutting."

"Oh, that sounds better. Good pay?" Doughboy said.

"Bottom dollar, minimum, you know," Jamaal said. "Getting some overtime now and then. That helps."

"Now, since you been out and about, you hear 'bout Pink?"

"Ain't heard nothin," Jamaal said.

"That little incident in the Q-Mart—things didn't go very well for him."

"How bad?" Jamaal asked.

"Maybe five to ten," Doughboy said. "Only good thing about that whole mess was he didn't actually shoot anybody. He's only got to deal with possession, and attempted robbery and the weapons charges. Bad, but it coulda been worse."

"Five to ten," Jamaal said. He was seeing the inside of the prison again. "Five to ten. Damn."

"Come with me," Doughboy said, as he walked up the block toward his usual outpost.

Jamaal went with him. Couldn't do any harm, he thought.

"You know, I got another fella comin' on soon. Getting out next week, actually. Gonna take Pink's place out here," Doughboy said. "But I do have another opening."

Doughboy turned the conversation to the weather, football, and spent a minute admiring two attractive women who walked by going the other way.

When he stopped his stroll, they were next to a car, parked just about in the same place Jamaal had been when he was busted. But this wasn't just any car. This was a brand-new Mercedes. Not the usual black, no, this machine was a deep, deep burgundy red. Rich brown leather inside.

"Oh," Doughboy said, acting like he had just noticed the vehicle. "Mmm, nice set of wheels."

Jamaal walked up to the car and inspected ... admired it.

"Damn," Jamaal said.

"Say, how 'bout you give it a test drive," Doughboy said. He pulled out a key fob, chirped open the doors and tossed the key to Jamaal. "Hop in."

Jamaal was sitting in the driver's seat, just feeling the touch of the leather on the steering wheel and shift lever. He touched the 'start' button. The instrument panel came to life. He couldn't hear the engine—just felt it idling through the steering wheel.

"Damn," Jamaal said.

Doughboy slid into the passenger seat next to Jamaal.

"Let's take a little ride," Doughboy said. "Let you get the feel of the machine you'll be drivin'. Like I said, I got this other job opening. Need a driver, take care of my new set of wheels here. Little chauffeur work and you take care of maintenance and do some detailing. Keep everything just so.

"Might have to make an occasional pickup or delivery," Doughboy continued. "All very respectable, high-class stuff though. Ain't sending this baby into any run-down neighborhoods."

Jamaal looked at two boarded-up storefronts and the huge vacant lot across the street and smiled just a little. Doughboy kept on talking.

"I'll make sure you get your time off—even work out some vacation time. Benefit plan is a little skimpy," he admitted. "No health insurance or nothin'. But you'll be earning about ten times what you make as a meat cutter, so you'll be able to afford whatever you need."

Jamaal smiled. His hand was on the shift lever. He dropped it into drive, but he still had his foot on the brake. Jamaal didn't say anything. He was thinking and thinking and thinking.

"Damn," he said, suddenly, and slipped the shift lever back into park. "No license," he said, turning toward Doughboy. "I completely forgot—since I was incarcerated, there were these tickets and stuff. I got some fines I gotta get cleared up and ... well ... with all that stuff, my license is suspended and maybe expired, and … well, you see, I can't take no driving job."

"What?" Doughboy said. "You giving a damn about a license? Half the guys do any driving round here for me ain't got no license. Since when …"

"Don't want to chance it," Jamaal said, cutting him off. "Still got a bunch of stuff to work through," he said, as he opened the door and got out of the car.

"And I'll tell you, man, I'm really disappointed. This car, it's beautiful and I would love to be drivin' it, but you know, one little slip up, and with my troubles—well you know that would cause issues for you and you don't need any problems like that."

Jamaal was talking fast and looking for a way to end the conversation.

"Damn, damn, damn," Jamaal said. "What time is it?"

"Close to six," Doughboy said. "You right. C'mon, let's go grab a bite …"

"I missed my appointment!" Jamaal said. "Damn, and they'll be waiting for me. Gotta go," he said, and started off at a run, toward the corner. He spotted a break in the traffic and sprinted across the street, then slowed to a jog as he went up Pine Street, heading in the general direction of Pacific Avenue. He didn't know where he was going at the moment. He was just getting away.

The Richest Man in New Babylon

Rule Number 3

J amaal had agreed to meet the Rev the next day.

"In front of the church," the Rev said. "Six thirty a.m.—gotta be early so you can get to your job."

The meetings with the old man and his friends were almost like a job, too. Jamaal wished he could skip to the end—arrange a meetup with the richest man so he could learn his secrets and start practicing the important part of his quest: accumulating some serious money and getting ahead. But he knew the old man had a plan, and he would have to play along with him if he wanted that final introduction.

Jamaal arrived five minutes early, but the Rev was already there waiting.

"Right across the street," the Rev said.

"Right across ..." Jamaal started. "You mean the daycare center? We're going to get financial advice from a bunch of babies?"

"I hadn't thought of it quite that way," the Rev said. Then he broke out his big toothy grin and said, "Yes," as they crossed the street.

Jamaal held the door for a woman who was hurrying into the center with one child in a carrier and a toddler in tow. He and the Rev followed her through a coat room into a big, kid-friendly reception area. Even at 6:30 in the morning, the place was hopping.

A tall African American woman in a business suit noticed the Rev and came over to embrace him warmly.

"Karen McDonald," the Rev said. "Jamaal Thomas. The young man I wanted you to allow to be an observer."

"Jamaal," Karen said, greeting him warmly.

"Ms. McDonald," he said, extending his hand.

"Call me Karen," she said.

"The Rev wants me to go over one of his rules with you," she said. "But first, you need to spend a little time watching the action."

She led Jamaal into a classroom with a half a dozen tiny kids—babies really—most of them crawling around.

"Just wait here," she said. "Watch what's going on. Keep an eye on the little girl over there, holding onto the edge of the table. Her name is Alysha. I'll be back in a few minutes."

Jamaal curled himself down into a chair that was only a foot or so off the floor and built for a three-year-old.

The little girl Karen pointed out, Alysha, was not doing anything remarkable. She was pulling herself up on a low plastic table and standing on two wobbly legs.

First, she would wobble around the table going one way and then wobble back the other way. After a bit, she started holding on with one hand, and she took two steps and then fell down on her well-padded butt. Then she pulled herself up to the table and did the same thing all over again.

Alysha ignored all the other kids and the teachers—there were two of them—in the room. She kept pulling herself up, staggering around a bit and then falling down.

One of the little crawling kids scooted over to where she was and bumped into her. She fell down, and they both laughed, but Alysha seemed more set on standing and wobbling than playing. So, she went back to doing that.

She was doing the one hand thing, and then she let go and took about three steps away from the table and stopped. She seemed really excited about the view—looked around and seemed surprised by it all. You could see she was going to fall over soon—just didn't know which way.

Boom, there she goes, Jamaal thought, butt first. Definitely the way to go, Jamaal thought, smiling. Nice soft landing.

Alysha crawled back to the table, pulled herself up and started the one hand thing. She took two more short walks, followed by soft landings.

Karen came back in the room and Jamaal stood up, still watching Alysha. The tiny girl balanced herself and got ready to take off on another trip.

"Persistent," he said to Karen. "She'll go two or three steps and hit the deck and come back and try again. And again."

They watched.

Alysha left the safety of the little table and started wobbly walking out into the room. And this time she kept going—eight, nine, maybe ten steps to another little table. When she reached the other table—without falling down—she looked back, all smiling and giggling and proud of herself.

"Wow," Jamaal said quietly. "She did it. Wow. Cool kid."

Karen led Jamaal back to an office where the Rev was waiting. It was nearly seven. Almost time for Jamaal to leave to get to work on time. Not much time for talking about rules, for getting rich and so on.

"Well, Jamaal," Karen started. "What did you observe?"

"Little kid—baby—learning how to walk, I guess," Jamaal said.

"Good," Karen said. "And what exactly was she doing?"

"You mean, trying to walk?" Jamaal said. "You know. She was toddling. And taking a step or two and falling down and doing it again."

"What exactly was she doing, when she let go of the edge of the table?" Karen said.

"She was takin' these teeny tiny baby steps."

"There you are, Reverend," Karen said. "Rule number … what number is it?"

"Three," the Rev said.

"Rule number three," Karen said.

"You can write it down," the Rev said.

Jamaal already had his notebook out.

"Teeny tiny baby steps," Karen said.

"Rule number three," Jamaal repeated. "Teeny tiny baby steps?"

Jamaal was saying the words, but he didn't sound like he was really understanding the meaning.

"You are at the start of a long journey," the Rev said. "You got lots of time—your entire life to get this thing with money right. You're just starting out like some of those little babies you were watching, so …"

"So," Jamaal said.

"So," the old man repeated.

"Take teeny tiny baby steps?" Jamaal said.

"You'll fall down, too," Karen said. "Prepare for that."

"Yeah," the Rev agreed. "There will be bumps in the road and you'll be falling further and won't be as well-padded as those little babies. You're gonna have to get used to picking yourself up to get going again.

"Here's the thing," the Rev continued. "Keep things short and simple to start off. KISS. Easy to remember."

"KISS?" Jamaal said. "Oh, I see, Keep it Short and Simple."

"Or, keep it simple, stupid. That's another way to lay it out," the Rev said. "Use what works best to remind yourself."

"KISS," Jamaal said, and smiled a bit. "Keep it simple, stupid. That sounds about right for me."

"And then—baby steps," the Rev said.

"Baby steps," Jamaal said. "Baby steps."

"That's right," the Rev said. "You want to be a millionaire some day?"

Jamaal paused, surprised by the question. "Sure," he said finally. "Why not?"

"Think about it. If you want to have a million dollars," the Rev said, "you gotta start off by having, say, a thousand dollars. And before you have a thousand dollars, you gotta have a hundred dollars.

"You start off thinking I got to save the million dollars—well that's a steep mountain to climb. Damn near impossible. But you ask yourself—'can I save a hundred dollars?' Sure, you can save a hundred dollars easy, right?"

"Hey, I already got ten bucks in the credit union," Jamaal said.

"Ten percent of the way home," the Rev said.

"That first ten dollars—that's a baby step," Karen said. "Next, may be just another ten dollars. You saw how little Alysha was learning, practicing the same thing again and again."

"Baby steps," Jamaal said.

"Alysha, she'll be walking all around the room in a week or two," Karen said. "Then running and, well, you know kids."

Jamaal smiled. "Yeah, I know. I got a daughter—three years old now. I know," he said.

"You're just starting out. Pulling up on the table. Taking baby steps," Karen said. "A little time and lots of practice, it won't be too long. You will be flying around yourself."

"Yeah," Jamaal said. "Yeah, I hope so."

THE RULES

1. PAY YOURSELF FIRST

2. IF YOU WANT TO HAVE MORE MONEY—
   SPEND LESS

3. TEENY TINY BABY STEPS
   KISS

Making the Best of It

A notice about a new job opening appeared on the bulletin board in the break room of the packing plant on Thursday: Assistant Plant Maintenance Engineer. Jamaal submitted his application for the job on Friday. Anything to get out from under the thumb of Mr. Arvin Parker, he thought.

Jamaal had spent more time in the library, using the "employment resources" Mrs. Ross had told him about.

Having a resumé now was a big deal. Most resumés list what job you had and when you had it. But except for some part-time jobs in fast food places that he had during high school, and the job at the packing plant now, Jamaal didn't have any employment history. At least he didn't have anything he could put on a resumé.

So instead of making up that kind of work history, he used a computer program that helped him make up a "functional" resumé. It listed all the skills he had, like driving, and doing brake jobs on cars and changing oil and some other kinds of repairs. His work in the packing house had given him more experience than he wanted in cleaning up stuff and "sanitizing" and handling waste disposal containers. He didn't enjoy doing much of that, but he wrote it down. He added stuff about being responsible and handling money and customer relationships. He couldn't say he was doing it for Doughboy's customers, but he had the experience and skills, so he figured he could write it down.

The Human Resources lady at the packing house told him he would get an interview. "Wednesday at two p.m.," she said. "Come here, to the HR office, and I'll escort you to the small conference room."

On Wednesday, Jamaal was on the cutting line. He told the shift leader he had an appointment with HR and went to the break room to change into his 'good' clothes. No suit and tie—he didn't have anything like that in his wardrobe, but he looked respectable. He arrived right on time, carrying two copies of the resumé in that composition notebook he was using to write out 'The Rules'.

Another guy, a Hispanic guy who worked on his shift, was coming out of the conference room. The HR lady signaled Jamaal to go in.

The man sitting at a small, round conference table with his back to the door was making notes about something. When Jamaal went around to find a seat, the man looked up and Jamaal was face to face with Mr. Arvin Parker.

Jamaal knew he didn't have a chance.

"You got a resumé?" Parker asked.

"Yes, sir," Jamaal said, pushing a copy of his resumé over to Parker. He already had Jamaal's application in front of him.

Parker was reading the resumé. He paused twice to look up at Jamaal and looked back down at the resumé. Then he grunted, put the papers down and looked at Jamaal.

"Now, what makes you think you'd be qualified for this job?" he said.

"Well, sir," Jamaal started. "I'm already doing a lot of the kinds of work in the job description, so I have experience. I've got a good mechanical aptitude so I know how to work with machines—do maintenance, check out problems and make repairs. I'm highly motivated. I get along pretty well with all the people on my shift.

"I know I'm not the fastest person on the line …" Jamaal started.

Parker snorted, muffling a laugh.

"… but I do have experience there, and so I have a good understanding of how everything works. And I'm real motivated, too. Got a lot to prove, and I'd like to show you the work I can do."

"Motivated?" Parker said. "So, with all that motivation, how come you are just about the slowest person doing the line work?"

"Don't know, sir," Jamaal said. "I'm just trying to go fast as I can without cutting myself. It ain't easy work."

"Oh, so you're looking for some nice, easy work now?" Parker said.

"I didn't mean it that way," Jamaal said.

"Stuff that won't take too long? Parker said. "So you can spend a little more time in the break room? Maybe take nice long lunch breaks, too?"

Jamaal knew it wasn't a good idea to say anything, now.

"This resumé of yours, doesn't say much about your employment history. Before you started here, where were you working?"

Jamaal paused before saying anything. He went through his options. This isn't a man you can BS, he thought.

"I was incarcerated, sir," he said.

"Here? In Northern State?" Parker said.

"Yes, sir," Jamaal said.

"Not supposed to ask, and you don't have to answer, but what were you in for?" Parker said.

"Drug charge," Jamaal said. "Possession with intent.

"I did a lot of maintenance work," Jamaal said quickly, trying to change the subject. "I can clear drains and unstop toilets, stuff like that. Floor polishing machine—spent a lot of time with that."

"And are you good and well and thoroughly rehabilitated?" Parker said.

He said that word like it was a kind of joke: re–ha–bilitated.

"I never did drugs myself," Jamaal said. "I was just working for a crew. Yes, sir, I'm rehabilitated."

"Humn," Parker paused. He was looking hard at Jamaal. "You had the look of a man who had just done some time. Maybe that's why I had my eye on you—give you a little special attention."

"Yes, sir," Jamaal said.

"Sometimes, a young man—a boy—can do stupid things," Parker said. "Dumb, stupid things."

"I know that," Jamaal said. "I mean, I really …"

Parker cut him off.

"You don't know the half of it, Jamaal. You just got a little taste of how terrible prison can be," Parker said. "I lost seven years of my life because I was young and stupid, like you. I had the misfortune of runnin' into a 'tough on crime' prosecutor who was gettin' ready to run for mayor. Lockin' up stupid black kids was part of his election campaign."

"I didn't know …" Jamaal started to say.

"I don't talk about it," Parker said. "But I do keep an eye out for young men such as yourself, who might need an extra kick in the butt to stay on course."

"You mean to tell me you ain't just a plain old SOB who enjoys making life miserable for me?" Jamaal said.

Parker smiled. He actually smiled.

"Well," he said. "There is just a little bit of that goin' on, too. Don't want to see you get too full or yourself."

Then Parker shifted gears.

"Okay, I have your application and your resumé. There are three or four more interviews, so it's gonna be a little while before we select a candidate or have follow-up interviews. Do you have any questions?"

"No, sir," Jamaal said.

"You will," Parker said. "Catch me when I'm out on the floor. Let me know what's on your mind."

Jamaal met the eyes of the man he had thought of as being his biggest enemy. But now, he seemed like ... well, something else. Maybe not a friend, but not an enemy.

"Like I said, we have a bunch more interviews," Parker said. "Probably won't have a decision until the end of next week."

"Okay, sir," Jamaal said, standing up and collecting his papers and notebook. "Thank you very much for your time. I appreciate your consideration."

Jamaal wrote a thank-you letter to Mr. Parker the next day, the way all the job hunting 'resources' recommended. He mailed it to *Attn: Mr. Arvin Parker* at the plant. Seemed ridiculous. He could just go in and hand it to the foreman. But sending in the mail was the right way to do it—that's what all the resources said.

Jamaal settled down to wait for the final word. He would have to think about this and worry for at least a week. But Parker surprised him three days later. Jamaal got the job.

His hours changed—he had to get to work an hour earlier. He got a little more money. And he had a lot better understanding about why his boss was being such a hard ass. He still minded it, but he didn't mind it nearly as much as he did before.

Sunday Dinner—Winter

Cold, cold, cold, Jamaal was thinking. He was lucky, though. The Rev advised him to hit the thrift stores before the cold weather set in. He was prepared when it hit.

He stomped the snow off his boots and peeled off his bulky jacket. He found room for the jacket, his scarf and his knit cap on some hooks on the big antique coat rack in the front hallway of Gunny's house.

Two minutes later, Jamaal, Gunny and the Rev were gathered around a big pot of chili on the dining room table.

"Don't much like all the cold and snow and stuff," Jamaal said, "but it did prove to be a fruitful business opportunity."

"How's that?" Gunny asked.

"After I shoveled out Jennifer, I went down to the hardware store on High Street and got me a decent shovel," Jamaal said. "Then, I got about three more houses on Oak Street—her neighbors, and maybe four more coming over to Pacific Avenue.

"The Rev took me on to clean up the stuff around the church that the plow company doesn't do.," He said, nodding at the old man. "Then he sent me over to the pastor's house, which I did for free, but he gave me a nice tip. And I got three more houses on that block. I was almost at your house, Gunny, when one of your neighbors flagged me down. Which is why I was running late.

"Nearly a hundred and fifty dollars," Jamaal said. "Lot better than a day at the packing house."

"Profitable day's work," the Rev said.

"Not all profit. Gotta take away the cost of the new shovel. And, I took three breaks—spent about fifteen bucks for coffee and food. But I'm gonna have more than a hundred to put in savings. Right? Rule number one? Pay yourself first?"

The old men smiled. The three of them chatted while doing serious damage to Gunny's chili. And there was cornbread, a green salad—Sunday dinner with Gunny was usually a pretty good feed.

Later on, in the kitchen, Gunny asked Jamaal how he was doing.

"I'm good," Jamaal said,

Gunny went on, "No, son, I want to know. How are you really doing?"

"It's hard," Jamaal said. "I feel like I'm just marching in place. Money comin' in, but it ... it's not enough. I feel good about paying Jennifer rent, now. She's letting me stay on, and I feel like I'm pulling my weight, and that's all a good thing. But it's like, instead of my bills going down, they're going up.

"I've only been putting five dollars in savings, most weeks," Jamaal continued. "And one week, I just put in one dollar. Pretty pathetic," he said.

"Actually," Gunny said. "I'm gonna disagree with you on that. You put one dollar in savings one week, hell son, that shows me you are actually 'getting' it. You're following up on your commitment—even though it's hard."

"And don't forget Rule Number Three," the Rev chimed in. "Baby steps. Little bit at a time to get started, and Jamaal, you're just getting started."

"Another thing to remember—I warned you about this—you're going to war," Gunny said. "You've got enemies out there, trying to defeat you. Get your money. Get you down. Get you depressed and make you want to quit.

"Sounds to me like you have been holding your own. You're building up a base of operations—got a place to stay with your sister. You've got a strategy—pay yourself first."

"And you know what—today you just won a battle," Gunny said. "You saw an opportunity, went out and busted your ass, and came up with a nice little, unexpected pay day. Not bad."

"Most impressive thing to me," the Rev said, "is that you're thinking about putting it into your savings. That says a lot about how you're doing, Jamaal."

"You're gettin' it, son," Gunny said. "Hang in there. Be strong. You are gettin' it."

Rule Number 4

"Notebook? Pen? You'll need them," the Rev said.
"Check," Jamaal said.

They were standing on the porch of a small house on the same block where Gunny lived. The Rev rang the bell. An elderly white woman opened the door.

"Miss Booth," the Rev said.

They entered the house, and the Rev gently hugged the older woman.

"Ezekiel," she said, "you are looking very well. How is your health?"

"Tolerable," the old man said. "Aches and pains."

"Oh, always," she said. And they went off down the hallway talking about getting old and the weather. They left Jamaal to follow along in their wake.

Soon, after the Rev apologized for a tardy introduction to Miss Elizabeth Booth, the three of them sat around a small table in one corner of her tidy kitchen.

Tea drinker, I'm guessing, thought Jamaal. And a minute later, Miss Booth was up and serving tea in delicate white cups. In the warm, bright light in the kitchen, Jamaal could see that Miss Booth was ancient—much older than the Rev. And she called him Ezekiel. That was strange. When Miss Booth returned to the table, the old man explained.

"This is one of the most important rules you're going to learn, Jamaal," he said. "You are going to have the good fortune to learn it from the person who taught it to me."

"Well, at least the mathematical aspects," Miss Booth said. "We didn't really go into finance."

"Compound interest," the Rev said. "That was all dollars and cents. And the problems we worked on were mostly about savings."

"The principles," Miss Booth said. "Yes, we were dealing with basic financial matters."

"Miss Booth was my math teacher, Jamaal," the Rev said. "Seventh and eighth grades, right down the block."

"Ezekiel was one of my best students," Miss Booth said. "His work was always precise with all the steps written down. This was before they allowed the students to use calculators and computers and such. Principles and process—that's what we taught."

"And taught it well," the Rev said.

"Tell me, Jamaal," she said. "How sharp are your math skills?"

"Well, pretty good, I guess."

"Addition and subtraction?" she said, "no problems there?"

"No problems."

"And interest calculations? Percentages?" Miss Booth continued.

"Well, I understand the idea. And I can figure stuff out like batting averages and free-throw shooting percentages," Jamaal said.

"That's a good start," Miss Booth said. "Compounding?"

"That's where you get some percentage of something—a small amount—and add it to the first number. Then when you calculate the percentage the next time the result is a little bigger," Jamaal said.

"Good," Miss Booth said. "Give me an example. Let's say for a savings account with interest compounded monthly."

"Okay," Jamaal said. "I got a savings account with $100 in it. And I'm getting five percent a month interest on that compounded monthly."

"Very wishful thinking," she said. "Go on."

"Well, after one month, I will earn five dollars. That gets added to my savings," Jamaal said. "Now I have $105."

Jamaal started putting the numbers down in his notebook.

"Next month, I'll get $5.25 in interest. Add that to the savings and I am at $110.25. Just keeps doing that—compounding."

"Very good," Miss Booth said. "You were paying attention in math class."

"Well, some," Jamaal said. "Plus, you better know how to figure stuff like that—out on the street. You can't do the math—some dudes can rip you off and you never know."

"Jamaal has some experience working as a small business entrepreneur," the Rev said.

"Oh, what kind of …?" Miss Booth said, and then, seeing the look on Jamaal's face, continued. "Let's not get distracted."

"We can agree then, earning interest—that's a good thing," Miss Booth said. "Earning compound interest, that's better."

"Now, what about *paying* interest?"

"That's where you can make some real money," Jamaal said. Miss Booth looked at him sharply. Jamaal smiled. "That is, if you are the dude makin' the loan.

"The interest—that's the vig on a street loan. Borrow a grand, you owe twelve hundred at the end of the week. Miss your payment—come up short—a man be visiting you, maybe with some friends or maybe just his gun."

"Oh …" Miss Booth said. "Well, it appears you have a good general understanding of the concept. Terms for a credit card are a little less drastic, but the same principles apply.

"A hundred years ago, the only things people involved in personal finance worried about were saving and compounding," Miss Booth continued. "They taught people to believe in the *magic* of compounding. And it was magical in a way. Back then, people could put money in a savings account and earn five percent compound interest.

"Today, the interest you can earn on a saving account isn't nearly that high," Miss Booth said. "You have to learn a great deal more about earning and paying interest if you want to have command of your finances. But the same fundamental principles still apply."

"So, here is a new 'rule' for you, as Ezekiel calls it," she continued.

Jamaal had already opened his notebook and was ready to write: rule number four.

"Never, ever, ever *pay* interest. Always *earn* interest," she said.

Jamaal finished writing and then started to speak. "But ..."

"No buts," she said. "The world of personal finance has gotten extremely complicated. Very smart, clever people are doing their very best to separate you from your money. Don't let them."

"But ..."

She cut him off.

"Make it a rule—a fundamental principle—never pay interest on anything," she said. She was spitting out the words. "Don't give away your hard-earned money. And don't give them the opportunity to confuse you with interest rates and fees and 'special' offers."

She paused, then continued more calmly.

"A minute ago, I mentioned the 'magic' of compounding interest," she said. "But today, people must be vigilant to avoid the 'evil' of compounding interest. Specifically, the evil of compound interest on credit cards."

Miss Booth was looking hard at Jamaal. She looked angry.

"So many young people today get in trouble with credit cards," she said. "These giant corporations make it so easy to spend money—just a quick swipe or a tap, or fill out a form online and you can have everything you want. Then, at the end of the month when the bill comes—that's when the young people realize how much they really spent. But the credit card companies still make it easy for them. 'Just make a small payment. We'll carry your balance, and all you have to do is pay a little interest on it.'"

Miss Booth was really getting worked up.

"A little interest!" she said. "You'll be lucky to earn one or two percent interest on your savings these days," she said. "But the same bank will charge you eighteen or twenty or twenty-one percent interest on your credit card balance. Compounded daily. Or more. In some states there is no legal limit to what they can charge.

"And if you miss a payment, they will charge you a penalty," she said. "If you don't pay your bill in full, they'll charge you interest on the penalty. And they may increase your interest rate.

"Call me old fashioned," she said, "but I think the entire business is terrible."

"But everybody uses credit cards." Jamaal finally had a chance to speak. "I mean, the Rev, Gunny. I've seen them buy stuff with credit cards."

"That's what is so frustrating about credit cards today. They are essential. You need them for online services and purchases. Stores encourage you to use them with extra rewards and discounts," Miss Booth said. "I use them myself."

"But," she said emphatically, "I never, never pay interest on my credit card accounts. When my credit card statement comes, I pay it off in full. I am following the rule ..."

"Never, never pay interest," Jamaal said.

"Correct," she said. "Even if you have a credit card—especially if you have a credit card—never, never *pay* interest."

She was calm again. But Jamaal could see how that business about credit card debt really upset her. Sounded like something he had to learn a lot more about, and an area where he had to be very, very careful.

"There is one exception to the rule about paying interest that we can discuss," Miss Booth continued. "There is one time when, with eyes wide open, you can consider paying interest. Do you know what I'm thinking about?"

"Student loans," Jamaal said. "Pay for going to school."

"That wasn't it," she said, then added, "so I might have to add another exception—but it would come with extra warnings, too. Can you give me another possibility?"

"Borrow money to buy a house?" Jamaal said.

"Correct," Miss Booth said, "a mortgage exception. And that comes with warnings, too.

"So," Miss Booth continued, "are you paying any interest now?"

Jamaal's face dropped. He looked profoundly sad.

"Yes, ma'am," he said. "I got …"

He stopped, looking at Miss Booth. He saw someone who seemed to care—who wanted to see him succeed. He looked into her gray eyes and made a decision. He continued.

"I was away for a while," he said. "Incarcerated."

"I've got prison fees and penalties, and fines from the DMV for some tickets I got driving, and they charge interest as soon as you're released. And I got back child support, and that's got interest, too. I got bills and interest up the yin-yang and out the wazoo.

"Oh," he stopped. "Sorry about that."

She was smiling.

"How much?" she said.

"Too much," he said. "I can't even count it. It's just too, too much."

"So, you're going to close your eyes and hope it goes away," she said mildly.

"I," he started. "I don't know."

"I've spoken with other young people in your situation," Miss Booth said. "They've told me how they feel. It's overwhelming. Almost too much to bear. They just wanted to close their eyes, hope it went away. And some of them—they just wanted to get high or get drunk."

"Yeah," Jamaal said. "Yeah, it's a lot like that."

"You have a pretty good understanding of interest and compounding," she said. "But I think you may need a refresher on addition and subtraction to go with it.

"Let's get to the bottom of this—see where you stand," Miss Booth said. "Let's meet again here in three days. Same time. And bring every scrap of paper you have with information about anything you owe."

Jamaal thought about what she said for a while.

"Okay," he said. "Okay," he said a little stronger, and then he felt a little different, too, like some sort of weight might be lifting.

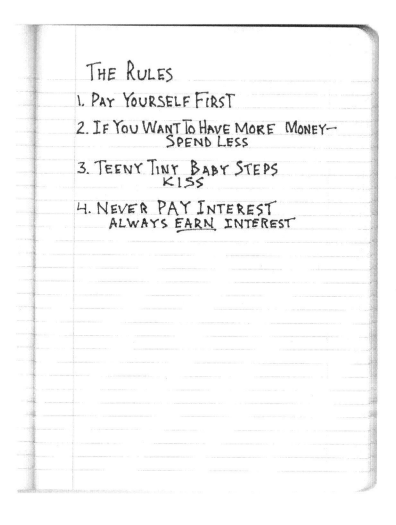

THE RULES

1. PAY YOURSELF FIRST

2. IF YOU WANT TO HAVE MORE MONEY—
   SPEND LESS

3. TEENY TINY BABY STEPS
   KISS

4. NEVER PAY INTEREST
   ALWAYS EARN INTEREST

Getting the Big Picture

Sunday. Football season. Jamaal found himself standing outside the Rent2Buy store on Broad Street—just a few blocks from his sister's house.

The one o'clock game had started and Jamaal saw a big play—looooong pass for a touchdown. And the replay of the throw. And replay of the catch. Six different angles. And it was just so crisp and clear and lifelike. Amazing.

Jamaal's sister had a TV, but it was old—a great big clunky box with a picture tube, not a flat screen. Jennifer didn't watch it much.

But if she had a TV like this, she'd watch it a lot more, Jamaal was thinking. That would be nice for her. And then maybe he could catch some sports …

Jamaal went into the store.

As soon as he walked in, a Rent2Buy salesman came right over. Except this wasn't any old sales "man."

"Hey there," she said, "I'm Shelia. Saw you outside, lookin' at the TV in the window. We've got a real nice selection of TVs right over here."

The slender, very attractive, young black woman led Jamaal over to a darkened section of the store. It was like being at the game—big screen, high def, and you could see the beads of sweat on the players' faces when they took their helmets off. One TV was more than a hundred inches wide—huge—like a stadium scoreboard.

While Jamaal admired the pictures, Sheila was explaining how easy it was to get a TV here.

"We don't require credit checks," she said. "You can return the set any time. And the best part is—it's so convenient. You pay a very low weekly rental. If you're happy with the set and you keep it, at the end of the rental term, you own it."

Jamaal was looking at another set now—one just about the same size as his sister's TV. Damn, Jamaal thought, only $7.99 a week—eight bucks.

"Where's the next size up?" he asked Sheila.

She took him to a fifty-five inch model on display in front of a couch.

"All the latest features," she was saying. "And this week only, we have a very special rate for it. Normally, it would be $14.99 per week, but for the next ten days, we have it for $11.99 per week.

"Just sign the agreement, pay twelve dollars and you can take it home today," she said.

Jamaal watched as a kickoff soared toward the end zone. The return man caught it and Jamaal could see every detail as he split two defenders perfectly, got a great block from one of his teammates and picked up another blocker and ... more than a hundred yards—a touchdown.

"I can get it today?" Jamaal said. "In time for the late game."

"We have it in stock," Sheila said.

"Damn—wait. I ain't got wheels ..."

"That's not a problem," Sheila said. "We have a truck right out back—the delivery team is ready and we deliver when you want—no waiting around."

"But, right now?" Jamaal said.

"Right now. Easy," Sheila said.

"What exactly do I have to do?" Jamaal said

"Just a little paperwork," Sheila said, leading him back to a cluster of desks in the back of the store,

She started working on her computer. She took Jamaal's name and address, entered the data and pressed a few keys. The little printer next to her started working.

"Here's your agreement," she said to Jamaal, sliding the pages toward him. She had highlighted several places and put little Xs there. "Initial this, this and this—then sign the last page and we'll pull your new TV out of our warehouse. As I said, we have it here in stock."

"You need initials for something—like what's this?" Jamaal asked.

"That's the breakage clause. It's just a formality. It says you acknowledge responsibly in the unlikely event that some physical damage occurs to the set."

"And if, like my sister gets ticked off at me and throws a dish and misses me but it hits the TV," Jamaal said.

"This clause acknowledges that you will pay for any costs above the accidental breakage threshold," Sheila continued. "That's the clause you initial here. The deductible is $500 or fifty percent of the buy-out price, whichever is less."

"Buy-out price?" Jamaal said. "What's that?"

"You can fulfill your contract any time—own the TV right away, if you pay the buy-out price. If you were in an ordinary store—one that isn't as convenient as Rent2Buy, it would be the retail price."

"Okay," Jamaal said. "And this?" he said, pointing the last place he was supposed to initial

"That's just an acknowledgment that applies to the effective interest rate—says you have reviewed all that information which you have—right here in the contact."

Interest. Interest? The word resonated in Jamaal's mind. Interest—rule number four—never, never, never pay …

"Well, if I'm not borrowing any money—just paying rent—what is there that's interest?" Jamaal said.

"This attachment—the appendix to the main agreement, discusses that," Sheila said.

"Tell me—what's it say? I'm not sure about what I'm looking at here. What's it say about interest?"

"It's just a formality—one of those government 'gotcha' or 'you gotta do this' things," Sheila said. "Really much more trouble than it's worth, but we have to go through the motions."

Jamaal was looking at Sheila now, and she was looking uncomfortable.

"Just explain it to me like I'm three years old," he said. "Interest. Am I paying interest if I sign this agreement?"

"No," Sheila said. "Just the rental fee."

Jamaal pulled the contract back toward himself and started a careful examination of the clause next to the spot that had been marked.

"Whereas the purchaser or representative of the purchaser …" It went on for two or three paragraphs, but Jamaal's eye was caught by one phrase: "… pursuant to the agreement, the effective interest rate of thirty three percent …"

"Wait a minute," Jamaal said. He put his index finger on the agreement. "This says 'thirty-three percent'?"

"It's a very unlikely scenario," Sheila said. "This clause only comes into effect on very rare occasions."

"It says thirty-three percent interest," Jamaal repeated, stabbing the contract with his index finger.

"Only on very rare occasions will …" Sheila was trying to move forward.

"Stop. Just wait a minute," Jamaal said, holding up the palm of his hand.

"Now, if I come in with cash money and buy that TV, how much will it cost?" he said.

"That would be $899," Sheila said.

Jamaal wrote the number down.

"And if I 'rent' the TV and keep it long enough to buy it, how much is that gonna be?" Jamaal asked.

Sheila took the contract and turned to the third page. Near the bottom, in a dense block of numbers, she pointed to a figure: $1,966.36.

Jamaal wrote down the second number.

"And now, if I subtract ..." Jamaal said as he worked the problem out on paper, "it looks like I'm paying ... wow ... I'd be paying $1,067.36. Shoot—that's even more than 33 percent interest ... more like 110 percent. The magic of compounding. Hell, more like the evil of compounding, just like Miss Booth said," he muttered out loud to himself.

"We have certain costs and fees, and the convenience of the rental ..." Sheila said.

But Jamaal was already on his feet and walking toward the door.

Never, never, never pay interest, he was thinking. Damn good rule—mess it up, you'll really be a fool.

Getting to the Bottom Line

Sitting at the little table again with cups of tea, Jamaal and Miss Booth sorted through the stack of papers Jamaal brought in a grocery bag. With help from the calculator Miss Booth provided, Jamaal listed all his outstanding debts—at least the ones he knew about. Now he was going over them all again to see what kind of interest or penalties he was facing.

"If you're not sure, take a guess and add it on," Miss Booth suggested as Jamaal searched on a bill from the motor vehicles commission for an interest rate. "Guess high," she said. "If you get a surprise, it's better to owe less than more."

After about an hour of sorting and checking and calculating interest rates, Jamaal looked at a column of thirteen numbers. He entered them on the calculator. After entering the last number, he pressed the "plus" key and stared at the result.

"Oh man—$15,315," he said. "Today anyway. Tomorrow it'll be more."

"How do you feel?" Miss Booth said.

"It's, it's just so much," Jamaal said. "I knew it was a lot, but … I mean, this is a lot. But to be honest, it's probably less than I thought it would be," he continued. "And at least now I know."

"Now you know," Miss Booth said.

"So now what?" Jamaal said. "Now what?" he repeated, shaking his head. "I've got a little more than $100 in the bank and I got more than $15,000 in debt. Now what?"

"You get to work," Miss Booth said. "You've got a problem. You go to work and solve the problem."

Jamaal shook his head and slumped down in his chair.

"Young man," she said sharply, using her 'pay attention in the classroom' teacher's voice.

"Yes, ma'am," Jamaal said. He sat up a little straighter in his chair.

"We will work out the math part of your problem right now," she said. "That will get you started. Then there's another important part of the 'get out of debt' problem that someone else is going to help you with.

"Now, let's get to work," she continued. "You can't pay all of your bills right now so which bill or bills are you going to pay first?"

"Well," Jamaal said. "I got to pay the DMV fines to get my license. I guess I should pay that first."

"Maybe," Miss Booth said. "You have a car?"

"No," Jamaal said, "but some jobs, you know, you got to drive."

"Good point," Miss Booth said. "Let's keep that in mind. What other choice could you make? What's in your best *interest*."

She said the word 'interest' with a little extra emphasis. Jamaal got the hint.

"Pay the bills with the highest interest first," he said.

"That makes the most sense, mathematically," she said. "See if you can come up with one other option."

Jamaal thought about it, but wasn't sure.

"Go over your rules," Miss Booth said.

"Pay yourself first," Jamaal said. "Want more money, spend less," he continued. "Teeny tiny baby steps." He stopped.

"Pay off this little one first," he said, pointing to the list. "Get rid of it. Cross it off."

"Another sound strategy," Miss Booth said. "Pay the smallest bills first so you can feel good about making progress."

"Okay," Jamaal said, "so which is it? Pay the smallest bill first? Pay the most expensive bill first? Pay off the fines that prevent me from doing any work that involves driving?"

"Very good," Miss Booth said. "Now you're in an excellent position. You seem to really understand your problem."

"Yes, but which …?"

"I'm just a retired math teacher," Miss Booth said, "not a financial advisor. I can only help you set up your problem. I can't solve it. That's up to you.

"But," she continued, "I do know someone else who can give you a little 'extra credit' lesson that may be very useful."

"The rich dude?" Jamaal said. "The richest man in town—like the Rev said?"

"No," Miss Booth said. "That is on Ezekiel's 'to do' list. But I have a former student who works downtown. He's had a great deal of experience dealing with people paying their bills. I think he could give you some very good advice. Are you interested?"

Jamaal said, "Yes."

Miss Booth made a phone call and, after going back and forth with Jamaal about his schedule, made an appointment for nine a.m. on Saturday.

Drive Shafts, Deadbeats and Dealing with Debt

Jamaal met Miss Booth promptly at nine o'clock at a busy intersection close to Jamaal's sister's house. Miss Booth was driving. Jamaal hopped in. Their destination: an auto parts store.

Action Auto Parts, Inc. was hopping. Cars jammed the parking lot with customers running in and out and lined up in front of every cash register.

Miss Booth, tiny next to the men—the customers were all men—was the most unlikely person in the store. But several employees seem to know her and soon she and Jamaal were ushered behind the counter, through a warehouse area and into an office suite.

A big, white man with a buzz cut and a firm handshake emerged from a corner office and greeted them. He said hello and embraced Miss Booth warmly and gently. Then he turned to Jamaal.

"Arnie," the man said, greeting Jamaal. "Arnie Swann."

Jamaal introduced himself and soon they were seated at a small conference table in one corner of Swann's large office.

Coffee, Jamaal thought to himself. And seconds later, Arnie Swann presented them with a tray, mugs, a pot of coffee, and some tempting baked goods. Jamaal smiled.

"Miss Booth has told me a little about you," Swann said, pouring coffee. "An accounting problem," he said. "Too many liabilities and not enough assets."

"Arnold was one of my best business students," Miss Booth said.

"Miss Booth taught two accounting classes," Swann said. "I took them and I was hooked. It fascinated me—seeing how all the messy details of a business could be translated into orderly columns on a balance sheet."

"My columns aren't so orderly," Jamaal said. "I'm not sure what you can do to help me. I just got too many bills and not enough money."

Swann laughed. "You'd be surprised. There were lots of times early on in this business when I was saying exactly the same thing.

"And my customers," Swann continued, "Jerome Browning—you know the name?"

"Big car dealer," Jamaal said. "I've seen him on TV."

"Started off with a little repair shop about the same time I started this business. We saw each other through some bumpy times. Jerry Wagner—you know him?"

"Sure," said Jamaal. "Supreme Automotive." Wagner had been a big-time athlete in high school until a bad knee injury. Now he sponsored local teams for kids and did stuff for the high school and ran a big, successful business.

"Jerry started out in his granddad's garage," Swann said. "Lots of liabilities. Not a lot of assets."

"I hear what you're saying," Jamaal said. "But I'm not in business. I'm just me, trying to get by."

"Maybe, maybe not," Swann said. "For now, let's say you are a business: Jamaal Thomas, Incorporated. You are the President, CEO, Chief Cook and Bottle Washer, and sole employee. Know what that means?"

"What …?" Jamaal was more than a little bit confused.

"You've got a very important job," Swann continued. "You have to manage this business of yours—Jamaal Thomas, Incorporated. Someone owes you money—that's a receivable. You have to be sure you get payment. You owe folks money—those are your accounts payable. Every good business takes care to manage those payables, too.

"Any business—you have to take great care to manage your receivables and your payables," Swann continued. "And if that sounds like it's all about money, it is."

"Yeah," Jamaal said. "Money, money, money."

"Now, let me change your mind about that," Swann said. "It's not about money."

"But you said …"

"It's about people," Swann said. "Personal relationships."

Jamaal looked puzzled.

"Jerome Browning, thirty years ago," Swann said. "We worked with each other. Found out we could trust each other. Grew our businesses together."

Jamaal nodded.

"Jerry," Swann continued, "when he started out, well, we shouldn't have let it happen, but, he ran up some pretty big bills. Got behind in paying them."

"Really?" Jamaal said.

"Really," Swann said. "But he was working hard, busting his butt and learning from his mistakes. We worked with him. And we learned we could trust him.

"Now he's one of our best customers," Swann continued. "That's how it is in a small business like this. You have to learn to accept some give-and-take and, bottom line, you have to learn to trust people. So now, big question for you, Jamaal Thomas, Incorporated, is this—can people trust you?"

"Well, sure …" Jamaal started to say.

"Seriously," Swann said. He was looking hard at Jamaal. Really hard. The big friendly guy was gone. Jamaal realized something different was going on.

"One of the hardest parts of a small business," Swann said, "is learning how to be a good bill collector. That's what I have to do to survive. If I don't collect my receivables, I'm out of business.

"Now, young man, you're in debt. So, let's look at that the way a business looks at it. There's a company you owe money to—a company that wants you to pay your bill so it can stay in business.

"Tell me about this debt of yours. Can you make it go away?"

"Go away?" Jamaal said. "How …"

"Simplest answer is bankruptcy," Swann said. "You owe me money because I was foolish enough to extend you a line of credit and I didn't collect your bill. Now you declare bankruptcy. I'm beat. You may not owe me anything."

"That sounds like a good thing …?"

"Might be. Might not," Swann said. "Bankruptcy is complicated—you need a lawyer—and no lawyer does a bankruptcy case without getting paid in advance because—you know—you're going through bankruptcy."

"So, you gotta have money to get out of paying money?" Jamaal said.

"Yeah, sort of like that. And it gets more complicated," Swann continued. "There are several types of bankruptcies," he said. "One kind, you promise to pay back everything and you get extra time. A kind of 'do-over'," he said. "Other kinds—you can get the debt 'discharged'—that's the legal term—just make it go away."

"So that's good," Jamaal said.

"Not necessarily," Swann said. "Any bankruptcy is going to follow you around. Anytime somebody checks you out—your credit report—they'll see that you declared bankruptcy. That goes on for ten years."

"So, that's not good," Jamaal said.

"Maybe," Swann said. "Maybe not.

"You go through bankruptcy, you've cleared your debt so now maybe you have money to do business with me," Swann said. "And there are rules that say you can't declare bankruptcy again right away. So, maybe I should work with you. Might be good for me. But maybe I'm ticked off because you beat me for money you owed me. So, maybe I'm not gonna work with you."

"Man, you're making my head hurt," Jamaal said.

"Good," Swann said. "You get in trouble with debt your head should hurt, at least a little bit.

"But listen up," Swann continued. "Yeah, this stuff is complicated. But you are smart young man. You know how to read and look stuff up on the Internet and so on, right?"

"Yeah," Jamaal said.

"Okay, as the Chairman and CEO and Accounts Payable Manager of You, Incorporated, here's what you have to figure out," Swann said. "How much do you owe? How much is the debt costing you in interest and penalties? That's the stuff you started doing with Miss Booth, right?"

Miss Booth, who had been sitting quietly, sipping her coffee throughout the men's entire conversation, nodded.

"Right," Jamaal said.

"Now, what are your options?" Swann said. "Bankruptcy, will that help? What kind of bankruptcy? Is it just another payment plan—or can you get the debt discharged?"

"Okay," Jamaal said. "But that means I won't have to pay you. Why would you want me to know about that?"

"I don't," Swann said. "If I'm holding your debt, I want you to think it's forever, at least until I get paid.

"What happens out on the street—you borrow money from some guy on the corner?" Swann asked.

"You pay it back," Jamaal said. "You pay it back when it's due or you get hurt real bad. And then you still gotta pay it back with a vig, or you get hurt even worse."

"Not a lot of options," Swann said. "Kind of stuff we're talking about, at least you have some options."

"Bankruptcy," Jamaal said. "Okay, I got to study up on bankruptcy."

"And there's another, much simpler option," Swann said.

"What?" Jamaal said.

"Figure out what happens if you just don't pay the bill."

"Just ignore stuff?" Jamaal said. "That's what I've been doing. I'm getting real good at that."

"I didn't say 'ignore'," Swann said. "I specifically said you should figure out the consequences of nonpayment. What happens if you don't pay?

"And you have to look at it two ways. What are the consequences for you personally? If you don't pay, maybe you get hounded by bill collectors but then maybe, after a while, they just shut up and go away. Or, if you don't pay, maybe it's something that can get you arrested again? Think. What are the consequences for you?

"And now, try to look at it from the other person's point of view. If Jamaal Thomas, Incorporated, fails to make a payment—how does that affect your bottom line. If this Jamaal Thomas owes you money and stops paying, do you have any serious leverage over him? Sure, you can send a bill collector after him—but if he just says he's broke and ignores that—what will happen to you? And from a business perspective, would it make sense to cut some sort of deal with this Jamaal Thomas business?

"Let's say that Jamaal Thomas Incorporated owes me $1,000. And let's say he is only paying ten dollars a month, and maybe he's going to stop paying, or maybe he's going to go through bankruptcy. What if Jamaal Thomas, Incorporated, comes over and offers me $500 to settle our debt? Would that be a good thing for me as a businessman?

"Could be," Swann continued. "And how would that work for Jamaal Thomas, Inc.? Keep him in business? Clear some debt off his books? Hell, I might even be willing to do business with him again. Probably be COD—cash on delivery—to start, but now that he's paid me what he owes me, we can start thinking about growing the business again."

"Okay," Jamaal said. "Let's suppose I do all that."

"All what," Swann said.

"I get a list of all my debts. Figure out interest and penalties and stuff. I look up everything about bankruptcy," Jamaal said.

"You can even go talk to a bankruptcy lawyer. A lot of them will meet with you the first time for free," Swann said. "They're looking for business. You can learn a lot in that first meeting."

"Yeah," Jamaal said. "That makes sense."

"Just don't sign anything," Swann said. "Go on."

"Okay, so I look at every bill I got to pay and figure out what happens to it if I go bankrupt or what happens if I ignore … sorry … just don't pay. I try to figure out what's gonna happen to me. Then I look at the bill from the point of view of the person I owe money to—what are they gonna think—what are they gonna do—how's it going to affect them. That's about it," Jamaal said.

"That's how you get started," Swann said. "Okay, that's it," he said, pushing his chair back from the table.

Jamaal realized the meeting was over.

"That's all?" Jamaal said.

"Oh no, there's more," Swann said. "A lot more. But you've got some work to do now. Start getting a clear understanding of this debt of yours."

"Miss Booth got you started. She helped you understand how much you owe and how much it's costing you with interest and penalties. That's first base.

"Now you are going to examine each bill carefully, like we said. Can you discharge it—just get rid of it legally? Can you ignore it? What's the worst thing that can happen? Treat all this like you are running a business. You're in charge. Get all that figured out and it will get you to second base," Swann said. "A good start—but only halfway to home."

"Then, what's next? Jamaal said.

"Do your homework," Swann said. "Meet me here again next week. Same time."

The Bill Collector

Jamaal arrived at the auto parts store five minutes early. That was a habit he picked up recently. The easiest way to be sure you are not late for something was to be early, he had decided.

Mr. Swann was at the counter talking to Jerry Wagner. He signaled Jamaal to come over.

"Good morning," Swann said. "You've met? Jerry, this is the young man I was telling you about."

"I was just one of the little kids back when you were playing," Jamaal said.

"Not so little anymore," Wagner said, shaking his hand. "Say—you listen carefully to what Arnie—Mr. Swann—has to say."

"I'm listening," Jamaal said, and turning to Swann he added, "and doing my homework."

Swann smiled and nodded

"Gotta go," Wagner said. "Shop is jammed. We need all hands on deck."

Turning to Jamaal he added, "You're a fortunate young man to have Mr. Swann here on your side. He helped me— so many ways—getting my business going."

"You're way too generous," Swann said. "I was just standing on the sideline doing a little cheering. Providing some encouragement. You're the man who made the plays."

"Thanks, coach," Wagner said. "You listen up, Jamaal. You got a really good man on your team," Wagner said as he scooped up two boxes and a bag and headed for the door.

Swann led Jamaal back to his office and served coffee as before.

"Okay. What did you learn, doing your homework?" Swann said as he sat down.

"Bankruptcy isn't really an option," Jamaal said. "Like you said, it's expensive. There are a bunch of rules now for people like me—you got to meet with financial counselors and of course they're working for the system—so they make you set up payment plans and such. Seems like— hard for me to believe it but—you gotta have a lot more debt than I have to make bankruptcy worthwhile.

"For the amount of debt I have, it wouldn't save that much," Jamaal continued. "And besides, a lot of my debt like fines and child support isn't even covered. I could go through bankruptcy and I'd still be owing most of what I do right now."

"Good information," Swann said. "What else did you learn."

"I got contact information for all the offices. I talked to a few people, but they didn't say much—just told me where to send money. One lady at the courts—she sounded nice—said there might be some charity group that would help with fines."

"Nice sounding lady—what's her name?" Swann asked.

"Ahh ..." Jamaal paused. "I didn't ask her."

"Jamaal," Swann said, "any time you're working on bills like this and you speak with someone who's helpful—you get the person's name."

"Yeah," Jamaal said, "I should have."

"Why?" Swann asked.

"Well, so I can get back in touch to ask more questions if I have them."

"Good reason," Swann said. "Any others?"

"Well, maybe she knows who to talk to about something else?" Jamaal said.

"Yup," Swann said. "In business we call that 'networking'. Remember what I said last time—it's not all about money—people and relationships are very important, too."

"Networking, huh?" Jamaal said. "Out on the street, you want to know who's got what kind of stuff and how much you can ask a guy who knows a guy. I guess we got networking."

Swann grimaced and smiled. "Yeah, basically, the same idea. This stuff you're dealing with now—digging out and managing your debt—it's a personal business. As much as you can, you want to get to know people so you've got someone to talk to—a person to deal with."

"Yeah," Jamaal said. "Okay. I get that."

"Learn anything else?" Swann said.

"Well, my biggest bill, you know, is for my child support," Jamaal said, "which is what they call 'arrears' in legal terms. According to the stuff I read about that, I may be able to have some of that reduced and maybe not have to pay all the interest.

"Another thing," Jamaal said. "You can go back and get payments reduced if you're not earning as much as you did before. I wasn't earning much before, but I'm worse off now. So that's the biggest thing I can work on—the child support arrears."

"And what are you doing about it?" Swann asked. "Are you making payments now?"

Jamaal paused before saying anything. "Not yet," he said.

The room was quiet for a while.

"Have you seen your ex?" Swann said, finally breaking the silence

"Not an ex," Jamaal said. "We were never married. She got real upset with me when I started working on the street. And when I got arrested, she didn't want anything to do with me."

"And you?" Swann said. "The child? Children? Do you care?"

"Child," Jamaal said. "Jameela, my daughter. She'll be three next month. She's special."

"And, you don't want anything to do with her?" Swann said.

"No," Jamaal said. "I mean, yes, of course I want to see her, but with her mom … it's really, really complicated."

"And you're not paying any child support, and you are in arrears and that makes it …"

"More complicated," Jamaal said. "More complicated."

They sat in silence for a while. Finally, Swann changed his tone from "disappointed" and got all businesslike.

"So," he said. "Time for me to get to work. Next week I'm going to bring in an expert to teach you how a man deals with his debts."

The Richest Man in New Babylon

Seven Steps for Dealing with Debt

For the third week in a row, Jamaal arrived at the auto parts store. Swann met him, took him back to his office and prepared coffee. This time, however, they were joined by a third man.

"Jamaal Thomas—meet LeRoy Williamson," Swann said. "LeRoy is my Senior Credit Manager. He keeps us in business by making sure that our customers pay their bills. If someone gets behind, he helps them catch up. I told him a little bit about your financial situation—I hope that's okay?"

Jamaal shrugged. "I need all the help I can get."

"Good. Pay attention. LeRoy knows what he's talking about," Swann said. He got up, picked up his coffee mug, and left the two men alone in his office.

"This won't take long," Williamson said. He spoke quickly. He was a man in a hurry.

Williamson was a good looking African-American man with a shaved head. He looked to be in his thirties, fit, wearing a suit and tie and he looked like he wanted to get down to business.

"Dealing with debt—it's not real complicated. You got a notebook, I see. Start writing. I've got like, seven minutes before I have an appointment with a customer. Seven minutes for seven steps to get your sorry butt out of debt."

Williamson was streetwise, no-nonsense, and had an attitude. Jamaal was a little offended by him. And a little impressed. He was definitely paying attention.

"First—you're in a hole," Williamson said. "What is it about ten K?"

"A little more," Jamaal said. "Maybe closer to fifteen."

"Step one for getting out of debt," Williamson said. "Stop digging. You're in a hole. Stop digging. No borrowing. And you don't spend a dime you don't absolutely have to spend."

"Step two. Man up. Face your problem, and if you're in debt, you've got a problem. Write it down, add it up and figure out exactly what you got to pay. All of it."

"I'm getting better at all of that stuff," Jamaal said, while Williamson paused to take a breath. "I'm doing all of that."

"Good," Williamson said. "Now, step three."

"Step three," Jamaal said writing.

"Step three. Pay *something* every time a bill comes due. Maybe you can't pay it all—maybe you can't pay what you said you'd pay—but pay something. On the street—you don't pay—really bad stuff can happen, right? You know that. You can get beat up real bad. You can even get dead.

"Business ain't quite like that, but a guy don't pay, he's in trouble. We got a word for someone who don't pay. Deadbeat. You may not be dead or beat up—but you are some kind of low life. A deadbeat. You want to be a deadbeat?"

"No," Jamaal said.

"Damn right. You don't want to be a deadbeat. Every time the bill comes around, you pay something," Williamson said. "Got that?"

"Yeah," Jamaal said.

"Step four," Williamson said. "Communicate. You got a problem. You're behind. That's when you get on the phone. Call me up and talk to me. In person—man to man. It's no damn fun, but you call me and talk to me. I'll know your name and who you are. Maybe I can help you out a bit.

"Maybe we can negotiate something. Maybe I can forgive some interest and late fees. Communicate with me. Be real. Be honest. Maybe something good will happen. At the very least I know that you ain't some kind of lowlife deadbeat.

"Step five," Williamson continued. "Prioritize. Mr. Swann, he said you talked about that. If I'm talking to you—I say pay my bill first.

"But you got a brain. And you got a pile of bills. Think, man. Figure out what's best for you. Pay little bills first, maybe get them out of the way. Start feeling like you're getting out from under. But don't ignore bills that have high interest or penalties. You're a smart kid. Work it out. Have a plan.

"Step six. Bust your ass. Work hard, get overtime if you can. Get a second job. Deliver newspapers. Pick up bottles and cans and return them for deposit. Scrape up every nickel you can, and do what?"

"What?" Jamaal reacted, surprised.

"Pay down your damn debt," Williamson said. "You take every bit of extra money you can get and pay down your debt.

"Time's nearly up," Williamson said. "Last step—you writing this down?"

"Yes, sir," Jamaal said.

"Repeat, repeat, repeat," Williamson said. "You got that?"

"Repeat, repeat, repeat," Jamaal said.

"Now, let me hear what you've got written down there," Williamson said.

Jamaal read back his notes on the "Seven Steps."

"Good," Williamson said.

"What about my credit score?" Jamaal said. "What do I have to do to take care of that. Make it better?"

"Credit score?" Williamson said. "It sounds like it's a big deal, right? It's not. Credit score is just a quick and easy way for some big company to decide if it's a safe bet for them to pile some more debt on you.

"Here's what you do to take care of your credit score," he continued. "Pay down your debt. Build up your savings. And pay your bills on time. Those are the most important things that go into a credit score," he said. "It's computers looking at data. They come up with a number. Just a lazy man's credit manager.

"But." He looked thoughtful for a moment. "There is one closely related thing to pay attention to. Your credit score is based on information the major credit bureaus have on file for you. You are entitled to see that information. Some time when you don't have anything else to do, you can go online and order up a copy of your credit report. It will be free.

"Now those credit bureaus—they want to make a profit. They will try like hell to sell you other stuff: credit protection and credit score improvement plans and all kinds of crap that you do not need. You ignore all that. Get a copy of your credit report and see if there's anything that's incorrect. Then, you can take steps to correct it.

"But listen—this is important—you don't need to pay anything to get your credit report and to get it corrected.

"There's three big credit report companies. Start with one of them and get things fixed. Then the next. Then the next. Truth of it is, none of this will make any real difference to you until you have all your debt problems cleared up. Then, if you go to get a mortgage or something like that, your credit score might matter. But for now, just ignore the score and correct the credit report if you have the time. And the most important thing: pay your bills on time. That's the best thing you can do," Williamson said.

"Okay, any more questions?"

Jamaal shook his head.

"Now that you have all this valuable information, put it to good use," Williamson said. "You've got the steps. Now do the work."

Then he paused. "One more thing," he said.

Jamaal focused on him.

"You need some help with this, you can call me," he said sliding a business card over to Jamaal.

"I got a clue. I've been inside—a long time ago. I got lucky and got a job with Mr. Swann here. Then I worked my ass off, and I made myself a little more luck. It's been a while now, but I got some understanding.

"When you get discouraged—and you *will* get discouraged—call me. I'll remind you it ain't impossible. Then I'll tell you to suck it up and get back to work."

Williamson rose and headed toward the door for his next appointment. He gave Jamaal a little tap on the shoulder as he passed by.

SEVEN STEPS FOR GETTING OUT OF DEBT

1. YOU'RE IN A HOLE. STOP DIGGING!

2. MAN UP. FACE IT. WRITE IT ALL DOWN.

3. PAY SOMETHING EVERY TIME A BILL COMES DUE

4. COMMUNICATE! MAYBE YOU CAN EVEN NEGOTIATE. DON'T BE A DEADBEAT!

5. PRIORITIZE. EVERYONE WANTS TO BE PAID FIRST. YOU HAVE TO DECIDE.

6. BUST YOUR ASS. GET OVERTIME. GET ANOTHER JOB

7. REPEAT. REPEAT. REPEAT.

HOW TO FIX YOUR CREDIT SCORE

1. PAY OFF DEBTS. GET CURRENT.

2. INCREASE YOUR SAVINGS.

3. PAY YOUR BILLS ON TIME!

More Work to Do

The following Saturday, Jamaal found himself at the parts store again at nine a.m. sharp. He didn't have an appointment, but he was there anyway.

Swann spotted him from behind the counter where he was chatting up a customer. A quick frown crossed his face, but it didn't stay there. When the customer left the store, Swann signaled to Jamaal to come over.

"Were we on for this morning?" he said, concern in his voice.

"Oh no, sir," Jamaal said. "I was just passing by. Seems I've been coming here so often, my feet just got on automatic."

"Oh, okay," Swann said. "I hate it when I mess up an appointment and …"

"No. No. Just passing through," Jamaal said.

"How's it going?" Swann asked.

"It's going," Jamaal said. "Step-by-step, like Mr. Williamson said. Feels like I'm just barely staying above water, but I'm alive and kicking."

"Beats the alternative," Swann said.

"I hope so," Jamaal said. "It ain't easy but so far I'm hanging in and I want to say thank you for the time you and Mr. Williamson took with me and all."

"Good," Swann said. "Now, as long as you're hanging around here, you want to make yourself useful?"

A curious expression crossed Jamaal's face. "Sure," he said.

"I got a man out sick in the warehouse and my team leader there can use an extra hand. Interested?"

Jamaal smiled. "Sure," he said.

"Just temp work," Swann said. "Minimum wage, but we give you a little bump for weekend hours. Got to do a little paperwork. You know your social?"

"Yes, sir," Jamaal said.

"All right, let's get you to work."

The Long List

Jamaal stared at the list—the long list. Too long, he thought, but now it was only twelve items long instead of thirteen. That was progress.

The extra money he was getting from working Saturdays at the parts store was a big help. He had increased his payments for the smallest bills and added some extra money to his child support. That was still the biggest bill where he was furthest behind.

He looked at the total for his DMV fine—a ticket for driving without his license—the smallest total on the list now. I could go into my savings, he thought, and pay it off. But that would pull his savings down under $100. No, he thought, not now. Jamaal liked having money in the bank—the savings balance was now close to $300.

He took the checks he had written and began addressing envelopes, getting them ready to mail. They were in order—smallest bill to biggest.

He stopped when he got to the last check—to Natalie.

It'd been six months now that he'd been sending her a check. They still had not communicated. But she had cashed the checks.

Maybe, he thought, maybe.

The rules and steps—all that stuff—communicate.

Maybe it's time, he thought.

Jamaal took out a clean sheet of paper and started writing.

A Letter to Natalie

Dear Natalie,

I am enclosing a check for child support. I know it is not the right amount, but it is all I can pay right now. With some old bills and some new ones that came up, I'm in a pretty deep hole with money. But I'm hoping things will get better.

I had some good news a few weeks ago when I got a second job at Action Auto Parts. That helped me put some more money in this check.

It would be a good idea for us to talk sometime about my support payments and arrears and all. I am going to be trying one hundred percent to pay my fair share. I was hoping that maybe we could make some adjustments to help me get caught up and make things right with you.

It would also be nice to see Jameela. With her being three years old and all, she must be quite a handful.

I'm living with my sister right now. We're getting along pretty good. We've ironed out some differences and I'm helping out with stuff and we're doing okay.

It would be nice to see you and Jameela some time.

If you're interested, you can write me at 27 Oak Street here in New Babylon. I don't have a phone yet, but I may have one soon. You can call and leave a message for me at the packing plant. I'm working there full time. Let me know your phone number and I can try to call you.

It may be the that best way to communicate with me is by e-mail. I check my e-mail pretty much every day that the library is open. My e-mail address is Jamaal103621@mymail.com.

Best regards to you and Jameela.

Sincerely,

Jamaal

The Richest Man in New Babylon

Rule Number 5

J amaal saw the Rev most Sundays. He had started attending the services at the big church on Pacific Avenue. It wasn't so much that he believed in all the religion stuff—Jamaal lived too much in the real world for that—but he liked the music and singing the old hymns. He liked the warm feeling people were sharing, even if he wasn't quite part of the group. He liked the peace and quiet in the big old building with the stained-glass windows. The old man was always around. Sometimes—most times—they'd have a cup of coffee afterward in the downstairs meeting hall.

Jamaal had gotten to know a few other people who attended the church. This particular day, the Rev had a new person with him.

"Jamaal, time for a new rule," the old man said as he walked up to him. "I want to introduce you to Angela McKenzie. Angela, this is the young man I was telling you about."

Jamaal shook hands with the woman. She was an African American woman, athletic, close-cropped hair, as tall as Jamaal with a firm handshake. There was something familiar. Then it clicked.

"Coach McKenzie," he said.

Angela McKenzie had led her high school to two state championships as a player, and then went on to an outstanding college career. She came back to the high school and coached the team to another state championship—and then went on to coach at higher levels. She now led a nationally ranked team at the State U.

"Jamaal," she said and retrieved her hand. "I've known Reverend Wright for quite a while now. I used to attend this church while he was pastor. He tells me you are a good prospect."

"Prospect?" Jamaal said.

"Yes," she said. "A 'project' as we say when talking about ballplayers. But you've got potential, he says."

"Project?" Jamaal said.

"A player with the physical tools—the height, the hops, the hand-eye coordination, but who still needs a lot of work, coaching and practice, to make the most of his ability."

"That makes me 'a project'?" he said.

"But still a good prospect, according to Reverend Wright."

"And that would be—to do what? I mean, you aren't recruiting for your team …?"

The Rev and Coach McKenzie both laughed.

"That would be quite a project," she said, "though I can put you in touch with the right people in the admissions and financial aid offices at the university when and if you're interested."

"No, son," the Rev said. "I was just telling Angela about your experience and how you've been working at getting things turned around moneywise and everywhere else. I told her I thought you were a real good prospect to succeed at—well, let's call it—the game of life."

"My entire approach to sports," Coach McKenzie said, "is that it's just one more way—one very good way—to prepare young people for success in the rest of their lives."

"When I saw Angela here today," the Rev said, "I thought maybe I could get her to share one more rule with you."

"This one is easy for me," Coach McKenzie said. "It won't take long."

They took cups of coffee into a small room off the main hall and sat in comfortable chairs. Coach McKenzie talked a little about her current team and its chances. Then she focused on Jamaal.

"Here is my philosophy about how to approach sports and life in one sentence," she said.

"This is a rule," the Rev said. "Write it down."

Jamaal got out his notebook and listened.

"Practice. Practice. Practice," she said. "Whatever you are doing, keep working at it, and strive to get a little bit better every day."

Then she paused and looked at Jamaal. After he finished writing, he looked up at her. She didn't say anything.

"Practice. Practice. Practice," he said.

She smiled. "There's so much in sports that you can't control," she said. "You may go up against better players. Get bad bounces. Have the refs miss calls. You can't control those things. And they will affect wins and losses.

"So," she continued, "what *can* you control?

"You can practice.

"Improve your preparation. Work on your fitness. Develop your concentration. Do your drills. Run your plays. Practice. Practice. Practice," she said.

"Focus your energy on the things you do have control of. 'Get a little bit better every day.' That's what I tell my team. We're focused on basketball, so we work on getting better at basketball skills: running our sets, playing defense, shooting free throws—you know—basketball stuff.

"It's the same thing in life," she said, "except in life, it takes a little more self-awareness.

"In hoops, you miss a free throw, you know it. You know what you have to work on.

"Living the rest of your life, that's more complicated, especially when you're both the player and the coach. You have to be very objective about what you're doing," she said. "What are your weak skills in life? What do you need to do to help yourself when you're managing your money?

Where do you put that energy—make an effort to improve yourself?"

"Well," Jamaal started, "doing stuff at work, I guess. Like my regular day job—working in the packing house— it's bad. Terrible. But I try to have a good attitude. I can try to do better."

"Any special skills they use there?" Coach McKenzie asked.

"There are some guys, they do some special jobs," Jamaal said

"Could you learn them?" Coach McKenzie asked.

"Have to ask," Jamaal said.

"So, that's a maybe," the coach said.

"Sharpening knives," Jamaal said. "That's a special skill."

"You could learn. Get a little better."

"Yeah, I think so," Jamaal said.

"What about new skills?"

"I do computer stuff at the library," Jamaal said. "I got an e-mail account now. That's good."

"Very good," she said. "Essential these days. Tell me what's next?"

"I'm not sure," Jamaal said.

"Then it's time to figure it out," Coach McKenzie said. "Get those next steps in sight. Pursue them. What kind of cook are you?"

"Cook?" Jamaal said. "I'm no kind of cook."

"You eat every day?"

"Well, yeah."

"So …"

"So, you're saying I should learn to be a cook?" Jamaal asked.

"No, I said the rule is—get a little bit better every day. And …"

"Cooking is …?" Jamaal was trying to follow her.

"Cooking is an opportunity to get a little bit better every day," Coach McKenzie said. "Oh," she added, "and free throws."

"You want me to get better shooting free throws?"

"Damn straight," she said. "You never know when you will have to step up to the line and make a big shot."

She was smiling.

"Getting a little bit better—you can always improve your discipline, your fitness, your emotional control, all the little things you need to do to be better at anything. And while you're at it—why not go ahead and work on your free throw shooting?"

Jamaal could tell that she was joking with him, and yet, she was serious, too. He knew all about shooting free throws—developing a routine. Step to the line, bounce the ball, rotate it so the seams feel right, lift your shot, follow through and watch it drop in. A routine—like making sure you save some money every time you get paid. A routine—like keeping all your bills in order and paying down your debt. A routine—like getting to every appointment on time or maybe a little bit early. A routine, yeah, maybe a new one, like going over to the school playground early evenings and working on shooting free throws.

Reverend Wright, Coach McKenzie, and Jamaal got up and collected their coffee cups.

"You know," Jamaal said, speaking to Coach McKenzie. "The Rev here, he started this whole thing telling me he's going to introduce me to the richest man in New Babylon. Now he has me meeting all kinds of interesting and important people such as yourself. And I really do appreciate this opportunity. But, now, since you've known the Rev for a long time, Coach McKenzie, do you think he's going to be able to introduce me to the top dude?"

The coach and the Rev both looked at Jamaal and smiled.

"Any time Reverend Wright made a promise to me," Coach McKenzie said, "he has always kept his word."

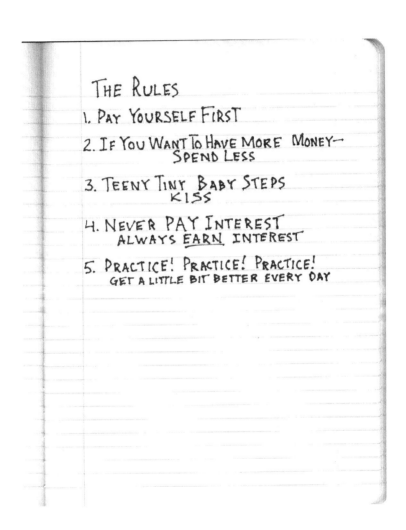

THE RULES
1. PAY YOURSELF FIRST
2. IF YOU WANT TO HAVE MORE MONEY— SPEND LESS
3. TEENY TINY BABY STEPS KISS
4. NEVER PAY INTEREST ALWAYS EARN INTEREST
5. PRACTICE! PRACTICE! PRACTICE! GET A LITTLE BIT BETTER EVERY DAY

A Cup of Coffee

J amaal had never much cared for coffee but he had been served it so often lately, he thought he was acquiring a taste for the stuff. He was thinking about coffee so he didn't have to think about Natalie, who was sitting in the booth in the Pacific Avenue Diner across from him.

Jamaal had received an e-mail message from her two days earlier. She had suggested meeting for a cup of coffee. He agreed.

Now what? They caught up a little—news about family. Natalie told him about Jameela—how incredibly smart she was, books she liked, games she played, food she refused to eat.

There was a lot of awkward silence, too. They ordered two desserts. She had cheesecake, and he had something real chocolaty. Made the coffee taste better, he thought. Jamaal paid, which accounted for all of his "go out and blow it" money for the week.

They were just getting up to leave, and Natalie stopped. She looked at him. Maybe for the first time that afternoon, she looked right at him.

"The support payments," she said. "The checks. I … ," she paused. "We appreciate them. I know it's hard now. You do what you can, okay?"

He met her eyes. "Okay," he said, nodding, still holding her eyes. "Okay."

Out of the Blue

The next day, as he arrived home from work, Jamaal's sister handed him a post office form. "I found it in the mail box," she said. "Some kind of official notice or something. You have to go to the post office to pick it up. Sign for it."

After waiting in line in the post office lobby, Jamaal got to a window, signed the slip, and gave it to the Asian woman behind the counter. She went into the back of the post office somewhere and now she was back with a big, official-looking envelope.

Jamaal took it and went out into the room with all the post office boxes. He put it down on a tall writing table and looked at it. The address said it was from D'Amico, Fratelli and Munzio, attorneys at law. Offices were in one of the big office buildings downtown. Jamaal stared at the envelope. Something told him he wouldn't find anything good inside.

"They want more than seven thousand dollars from me," Jamaal said to Jennifer when he got back home. "More than seven thousand damn dollars.

"Storage fees—that's what most of it is," Jamaal paced, caught up inside with a mixture of anger and frustration and … well … there was something so ridiculous about this it was almost funny. Almost.

"After they arrested me, they found my car, and it wasn't in a legal spot, and so they started ticketing it," Jamaal said. "Now I've almost paid all that off."

"But then the cops had it towed. That was a hundred and fifty," he said, pointing to a figure in the sheaf of papers he was holding.

"The tow operator—Magliozzi Brothers—they got the car and they charge a storage fee. It's twenty-five dollars. Not much, not so bad, except that's twenty-five dollars a day—for 300 days. Get that—300 days. That's like $7,500. And I'm incarcerated and don't know about this, so I can't do anything about it.

"And then, after 300 days and I didn't claim the car, they sell the damn car at auction. They got $200. They give me credit for that here," he said, pointing at the paper again.

"But they added another towing fee here. And here they got taxes, some damn service charge and interest. Nearly eight thousand dollars," Jamaal said, finally slumping it a soft chair. "I'm just starting to clear a little bit of my debt and … eight thousand dollars. And with all of that, I still ain't got no wheels."

Jamaal laughed. It wasn't funny, but what else could you do.

Looking for Answers

After a difficult night's sleep, Jamaal's head began to clear. He remembered LeRoy Williamson's offer. Jamaal called the auto parts store from the phone in the break room at the plant and asked for the credit manager. Williamson told him to come right over, as soon as he could.

The wave of anxiety and frustration Jamaal felt when he first opened the envelope had begun to recede. He was definitely thinking more clearly today.

LeRoy Williamson was taking his time, going through the papers. As Jamaal watched an expert comb through the documents, he even began to feel a little hopeful. Maybe there was a way out of this mess.

"So—you're dealing with debt, what's the first thing you do?" Williamson said when he finally looked up at Jamaal.

"Stop digging," Jamaal said. "This here though, it's from out of the past."

"Step two?" Williamson said.

"Man up," Jamaal said. "But you tell me—you gonna 'man up' to a debt when you never signed up for it or anything? Never had a warning? Nothing?"

"I'm kind of seeing this situation your way," Williamson said. "Not sure I'd be ready to start paying anything on this one, at least for now."

"So, we skip step three—'pay something'?" Jamaal said.

"For now," Williamson said. "On to step four."

"Communicate," Jamaal replied. "Get in touch. Talk to 'em, even if they are a bunch of scum trying to rip you off."

Williamson barked a quick laugh and smiled.

"What did you find out?" Williamson asked.

"The towing operation is close to the packing house, so I stopped in to talk before I came over here," Jamaal said. "Didn't take long. I explained how I was incarcerated and never heard anything about my car getting towed. Guy I talked to—name of Tony—fat white guy—seemed to be the dispatcher but he also seemed to be pretty much in charge—he said that was a real bad break.

"Then I said, since I didn't know about any of this, and they sold my car and all, that I shouldn't be getting this bill."

Williamson interrupted him.

"And he said, 'You're right, Jamaal. Just tear up that order to appear in court. We'll make it all go away, no problem.' He said something like that?" Williamson said, with a grim smile.

"No. Nothing like that," Jamaal said. "He just said he'd make it easy for me. He offered a 'settlement'."

"Humn. Interesting," Williamson said. "What kind of terms?"

"He said they could settle the debt for five thousand dollars. They would take payments. Charge me eleven point nine percent interest. He had the paperwork all drawn up. My name on it and everything."

"Paperwork for a settlement?" Williamson said. "Had it already prepared? You didn't sign anything, did you?"

"No, sir," Jamaal replied. "I figured that it was the beginning of some kind of bargaining. Can you tell me what you think?"

Williamson sat back quietly for a minute, steepling his fingers.

"I think the whole business sounds suspicious," Williamson finally said. "Got that paperwork ready in advance. Sounds like they've done the same thing before. Maybe a lot. Sounds like it's some kind of setup or scam."

"Any ideas about what to do? How to handle it?"

"A couple," Williamson said.

"You could just ignore them. What's the worst case if you just refuse to pay anything?"

"Not sure," Jamaal said.

"They could set out bill collectors on you. That would be annoying. But they don't have any legal leverage that I can see," Williamson said.

"Being as they are in the automotive business, there's got to be a big overlap between their customers and people we work with," Williamson continued. "If I let a few people know what's going on, these guys—Magliozzi Brothers—they'd feel the pinch. It's a tight community. Probably make them go away.

"But there's another possibility I think might be even better," Williamson said. "Let's make a copy of these papers," he said, carrying them to a copying machine. "I've got a friend who's an attorney. I'd like to have her take a look at them. And maybe ..."

"Go on," Jamaal said, as he followed the credit manager. "Maybe what?"

"Maybe you should take these SOBs to court. Sue them in small claims court for damages and screwing around with your vehicle—selling it without your consent. Like I said, I need to get a lawyer to look at this situation."

"You're thinking I should go to court with them?" Jamaal said. "Sounds crazy."

"No, not really. I go to small claims court quite a bit, working on the debt collection side," Williamson said. "Stuff I deal with is all pretty straightforward, cut and dried. I have everything documented."

"I'm a convicted felon, man, they ain't gonna listen to me," Jamaal said.

"You've got rights, just like anyone else. They'll listen to you," Williamson said. "Only two judges in small claims. Neither one of them likes to see people get jerked around. They got a lot a latitude. They work to get things right."

"So, you think I oughta …"

"Sue the bastards," Williamson said. "They want to take advantage of a man who's trying to get his life together. Sounds like this may be something they do all the time. They may even be working with someone inside the police department to set people up."

"Damn," Jamaal said. "Sue the bastards."

That sounded good.

Rule Number 6

The Rev was waiting for him outside Comp-Tech, a little computer store on Pacific Avenue, two blocks up from the church. A very slim black man wearing black slacks, a white polo shirt with his company logo, and gold, wire-rimmed glasses greeted them at the door. They went inside and the Rev made the introductions.

"Lawrence Barnes," the Rev said, "this is Jamaal Thomas, the young man I was telling you about."

"Jamaal, Lawrence here is a computer genius. He keeps all our church computers running, fixes anything, and unscrews all my technical screw ups."

"I am just your friendly neighborhood geek," Barnes said, shaking Jamaal's hand. Jamaal heard the trace of an accent in his voice. From the Islands, he thought.

"I like playing with electronic toys and I have been lucky enough to get a little business going," Barnes said.

Jamaal looked around. The shop was all neat and businesslike. Barnes ushered them into an office in the back that was lined with monitors. He saw computers, game stations, printers and all kinds of electronic gadgets on the shelves with everything neatly tagged and organized.

"Diet Coke?" he offered, pointing to a mini fridge. "Oh, and there is coffee up front." He pointed to a monitor and zoomed a camera in to a close-up of a coffee station close to the front door.

"I'm good," the Rev said.

"Same here," Jamaal said.

"Great," Barnes said. "The Rev asked me to share my wisdom—such as it is—on the subject of handling money."

"Okay," Jamaal said.

"My philosophy for handling money is really more about my philosophy for not handling money," Barnes said.

Jamaal looked puzzled. "This is a rule," the Rev said. "You're going to want to write this down."

Jamaal looked at his notebook. "We're up to rule number six," he said, nodding at the old man.

"This is short and simple," Barnes said, "three words."

"Rule number six," Jamaal said, writing in his notebook.

"Make it automatic," Barnes said.

"Make it automatic," Jamaal repeated, then paused. "What is 'it'?"

"Anything and everything that has to do with money. Treat money like in some kind of dirty, polluted, filthy stuff—which it actually is—full of germs and microbes and icky stuff. The smart thing to do is to keep your hands off it," he continued. "Make everything happen automatically."

"Make it automatic," Jamaal repeated, writing in his notebook.

"Set it and forget it," Barnes said.

"What kind of stuff are you talkin' about?" Jamaal asked.

"Here are some of the best opportunities—things that can become automatic," Barnes said.

"Direct deposit. That is where—instead of giving you a paper check—your employer deposits your pay electronically directly into your bank account. If your employer offers it, you should be using it. Direct deposit. Write that down.

"Online banking," Barnes continued. "Any full-service bank or credit union should offer online banking. If yours does not, find a new bank or credit union. Be sure it offers online banking. When you have access to online banking, use it. Online banking. Write that down."

"I got a credit union account," Jamaal said.

"Good," Barnes said. "Credit unions offer more service at lower cost than big commercial banks. And you will find, when you have direct deposit, you get even more benefits.

"Automate your savings," Barnes continued with his list. "Your online banking will let you do that. You can set up an automatic transfer. Every time they deposit your pay, you can automatically transfer money from your checking account and put it in your savings account. Then *you* do not have to think about it. The online banking system does it for you. Set it and forget it."

"Pay yourself first," Jamaal said, mostly to himself as he was writing. "Follow rule number one. Use online banking. Make it automatic."

"Another important service—online bill payment," Barnes continued. He was just getting warmed up to the subject. "You make sure you have that. You set up payment information one time for people you have to pay—name, address, account number—that kind of data. Then, when it is time to make a payment, you go online, enter the amount to pay and select the date you want the payment made. Click to schedule the payment. Your task is complete.

"Another benefit that comes with paying bills online," Barnes said. "You can set up payments to repeat automatically. This works well when you have a payment—the same amount every time—that you make regularly—every month, for example. Consider the rent I pay for this shop. I have everything set up—my landlord's name and address and the amount to pay. I schedule the payment. It goes out on the first of every month. Same amount every time. I do not have to think about it—it all happens automatically."

Jamaal was writing quickly.

"More automatic saving," Barnes continued. "Do you have a 401(k) plan where you work?"

"Don't know," Jamaal said.

"Find out," Barnes said. "It is not nearly as good as a pension, but these days it's what most companies offer to help you save for retirement. Do you know how a 401(k) plan works?"

"Ah …" Jamaal started to answer, then stopped. "No, not really."

"Excellent answer," Barnes said. "It takes a wise man to know when he does not know enough to bluff. Look it up online," Barnes continued. "You will find plenty of information. Then we will have a quiz."

"I'm not sure …" Jamaal started to say, but Barnes kept talking.

"Make it automatic. That is the rule. Now, why is this important?" Barnes paused briefly, but didn't really give Jamaal time to answer.

"First, it is easier," Barnes said. "Set it and forget it. Make a good decision one time and that good decision keeps getting repeated every 'next' time.

"Second, it is faster and more efficient. When you have everything set up, it will only take a few minutes to pay all your bills and manage your savings.

"Third, and for a lot of people in your position—being in debt and digging out of it—this is the most important point. You keep your hands off your money," Barnes said. "That has a big benefit. If you do not have cash in your hands, you do not go out and spend it."

"But man, it's my money," Jamaal said.

"That is correct," Barnes said. "It is your money—as long as you do not go spending it. Do you want to keep it, hold on to most of that money you worked so hard to earn?"

"Well, sure, but ..." Jamaal started to say.

"Then keep your hands off it," Barnes said. "Make it automatic—automate everything you can. Do not keep cash in your wallet that you can spend on things you did not plan to buy. And besides," Barnes added, "it really is dirty, filthy stuff—full of germs."

"But ..." Jamaal started.

"That is one of your rules, right?" Barnes said. "You want to have more money? Spend less?"

"Yes, but ..."

"Avoid temptation. Take advantage of technology," Barnes said. "When it comes to handling money, what do you want to do?"

"Make it automatic?" Jamaal said.

"That is the rule," Barnes said. "Make it all automatic—as much as you can. Let computers do the work for you."

"Make it automatic," Jamaal said.

THE RULES

1. PAY YOURSELF FIRST

2. IF YOU WANT TO HAVE MORE MONEY—
SPEND LESS

3. TEENY TINY BABY STEPS
KISS

4. NEVER PAY INTEREST
ALWAYS EARN INTEREST

5. PRACTICE! PRACTICE! PRACTICE!
GET A LITTLE BIT BETTER EVERY DAY

6. MAKE IT AUTOMATIC

The 401(k) Quiz

One week later, Jamaal was back at Comp-Tech, telling Barnes about a few changes he had made.

"Direct deposit," he said. "I signed up for that. It starts next week. And I'm all over that online banking. Got all my stuff set up. And you know what? It saves money on account of I don't have to buy stamps and envelopes to mail checks to people. It's cool," Jamaal said.

"Told you so," Barnes said.

"I got an ATM card so now I can get cash, and there's no fee for that at the credit union."

"Watch out for fees anywhere else, though," Barnes said. "Be careful with that."

"I got checking and savings accounts, so I set up for an automatic transfer," Jamaal said. "Pay yourself first—rule number one—now every week it automatically transfers my savings money from checking to savings. And I can log in any time and see my balance. It's cool."

"Make it automatic," Barnes said.

"Make it automatic," Jamaal replied.

"Now, that quiz," Barnes continued.

"Quiz?" Jamaal said, looking puzzled.

"You've got a little more automating to do—the 401(k) information," Barnes said.

"Oh," Jamaal said, remembering the conversation. "It's the 'what is a 401(k)' quiz?"

"Let's see how much you know now," Barnes said. "Then we can fill in the blanks."

Barnes handed Jamaal a sheet of paper.

401(k) Quiz

A "401(k) Plan" is a special savings program that many companies today offer. The 401(k) plan (and similar plans like the 403(b)) are named after sections of the US tax code. These savings plans have largely replaced pensions as a way for company employees to save for retirement. Test your knowledge about these types of savings plans by answering these true/false questions. The answers are in the back of this book.

1) In addition to saving for retirement, your 401(k) plan is also a good way to save for education expenses. T / F

2) Employers are required to match employee contributions up to a minimum of two percent. T / F

3) A 401(k) plan is "tax advantaged." This means that you don't have to pay any taxes on contributions to your 401(k) plan. T / F

4) If you take a job at a different company, you are required to close your current 401(k) plan and enroll in a new one at your new company if it offers one. T / F

5) All the money you contribute to your 401(k) plan is guaranteed to be yours to keep. T / F

6) All the money your employer contributes to your 401(k) plan is guaranteed to be yours to keep. T / F

7) If you have a particular stock you want to buy, you can specify that in your 401(k) plan investments. T / F

8) If your employer's stock is included in your 401(k) options, you are required to allot twenty percent of your fund to it. T / F

9) One good thing about a 401(k) plan is that there are no investment fees or additional costs. T / F

10) It is sound financial advice—a good idea—to enroll in a 401(k) plan if your employer offers one with a matching contribution, and contribute as much as the employer is willing to match. T / F

One week later, Jamaal stopped in to see Barnes. He was thinking about buying an inexpensive computer so that was a good reason to talk to an expert, he thought. Barnes was in the shop, and he reminded Jamaal about their conversation about 401(k) plans.

"The packing company offers a 401(k) with a two percent match," Jamaal said. "I'm signed up for it but only for the two percent now. I got a lot of other payments and my regular savings—pay yourself first—so I'm doing that. I'll look at increasing the 401(k) contribution when I'm out from under all this debt I still have."

"That sounds quite practical," Barnes said.

"Make it automatic," Jamaal said.

Barnes laughed. "Make it automatic."

"I am thinking about making a little investment in technology," Jamaal said. "I'm looking for a computer. Nothing fancy. Just something I can used for web browsing and online banking."

"You may be in luck," Barnes said. "I do have this little desktop computer—about five years old. Obsolete for my purposes, but it is still reasonably functional. Interested?"

"How much?" Jamaal asked.

"No charge," Barnes said. "But you will need a monitor. I have a pre-owned, 17-inch LCD unit you can purchase for twenty five dollars."

Jamaal smiled. "Cheapskate like me, you think I'm gonna pay twenty five dollars for some old piece of junk, used monitor. Maybe I can give you ten for it."

"Fifteen," Barnes said.

"Fifteen, huh? And you're including the mouse and keyboard and all the cables and stuff I need?"

"All included," Barnes said.

"You got a deal," Jamaal said.

The Richest Man in New Babylon

Another Day in Court

"And you made every effort to communicate with Mr. Thomas, concerning the location of his vehicle and its disposition?"

Judge Herbert Rosen, known to people who frequented the small claims court as "Hardass Herb," stared down at Louis Magliozzi.

"Well, of course, your honor," Magliozzi said. "Every effort."

"Can you show me the documentation?" Judge Rosen said. "The record of your communication with Mr. Thomas."

"Why yes, sir," Magliozzi said. He opened a file folder and gave the judge a copy of the legal documents that Jamaal had received.

"Your notification of the charges and—I see a certified mail receipt—one month ago—this year," the judge said. "And the additional communication? Your earlier efforts to contact him?"

"Well, that was done primarily by telephone," Magliozzi said. "We made dozens of calls—left messages."

"Great. Can you show me phone records? Call logs? Dates and times?"

Magliozzi was sweating, and the courtroom wasn't very warm.

"Uh, no your honor," he said. "We were just pursuing our normal business practices. I mean most of the time, when someone has a vehicle impounded, they get in touch with us."

"And Mr. Thomas didn't do that?" the judge said.

"Ahh, no …"

"Because he was incarcerated," the judge said.

"Well, we didn't know that," Magliozzi said.

"All the calls you made to try to reach him, and nobody told you that he was incarcerated?"

"Ahh, no ..."

"All the calls you made, and nobody mentioned that he was having these legal difficulties?"

"Ahh, we tried ..."

"Oh, I'm sure you tried," the judge said. "But here's the curious thing. Going back more than a year, you had no idea that this young man was incarcerated. You had no idea how to find him. You couldn't locate him to tell him what had happened to his vehicle.

"And yet, a month ago, you suddenly were able to locate him. You had his address—knew exactly where he was living. Now, how did that happen?"

"Well, we ... we did more follow up ..."

"Can you show me records of your follow up?" the judge said.

"Umm, not really ..."

"You have no records because you didn't really do any follow up," the judge said. "No, you have someone in the judicial system—someone who is working with you in your little scam, who is tipping you off. Someone who told you that one of your victims had been released and told you exactly where to find him."

"Your honor—"

The judge cut him off.

"I'm referring all the facts in this matter to the office of the District Attorney," Judge Rosen said. "In the meantime, if I hear about any other cases where you are attempting to run this scam on people who have been incarcerated, you can be sure I will weigh in with all the authority I have at my disposal to be sure you never do it again.

"Do you have a city towing contract?" the judge asked.

"Uh, yes, sir," Magliozzi said.

"If I hear one word about this kind of thing happening again, I will call in every political favor I have to be sure you don't have a contract. Do I make myself clear?"

"Yes, sir," Magliozzi said.

"Step back from the bench," the judge said.

"Mr. Thomas," he continued.

Jamaal stood up. "Yes, sir," he said.

"Earlier, when your friends here in court spoke on behalf of your character, I was impressed."

Jamaal turned and looked at the people in the first row of the spectator seats; Mr. Swann, Miss Booth and Mr. Williamson.

"I've known Arnie—Mr. Swann—since we were in grade school. We both had Miss Booth for math. I was not, unfortunately, nearly as good with numbers as Arnie, but she managed to drill enough into my thick skull to survive.

"Jamaal, you've got some really good people in your corner. You made some mistakes. You paid a price. That's over. What I see now is a man with a plan, and some very good people standing behind him.

"Don't let them down, son. Don't let us down. You may be seated."

Jamaal sat down, and the judge continued.

"Justice is now, and has forever been … imperfect. We try to protect the public, to deter criminals who would take advantage of of honest citizens—to punish people who break the law. But when someone makes a mistake, and is punished—that punishment is supposed to end.

"Do the crime, you do the time—that's what they say. But when you finish the time—it's supposed to be over.

"But somehow, in our criminal justice system, we've managed to find ways to make the people we punish keep on paying. That's not right. It needs to stop.

"Looking at the facts of this case, it disturbs me greatly that anyone would single out a young man who has 'done the time'—and target him in a scheme that smells of extortion.

"The court finds for the plaintiff and orders $500 in restitution for time and … well for … aggravation. The court also orders the defendant to repay the plaintiff the $200 received for his vehicle. The defendant will also pay $350 in court costs," Judge Rosen concluded.

He snapped his gavel down.

"Next case."

Sunday Dinner—Spring

Jamaal arrived at Gunny's house early. It was one of their Sunday dinner nights—the Rev was in charge and he was bringing Chinese take-out from the Szechuan Kitchen up on the avenue.

Jamaal stepped up on the porch and was just about to ring the bell when he saw someone's big backside facing him in the flowerbed next to the porch steps.

"Gunny?" Jamaal said.

The big man was up on his feet and shaking dirt off his pants. He still had his knee pads on, though, and he was looking pretty much like your average gardener's assistant.

"Jamaal," he said. "Didn't hear you coming up the walk."

"What's happening?" Jamaal said.

"Bulbs," Gunny said. "Putting in a few new ones, but mostly digging up some of the established plants, separating and re-planting them.

"I've always been partial to perennials of all types—flowers that you plant once and they come back year after year. Long-standing relationships. Get to know them. But they require maintenance. Can't just leave them alone. They require a certain amount of nurturing."

Gunny was on the porch now, putting away his gardening tools.

"So how are you doing? Any news?" he asked.

"News? Not really," Jamaal said. "Except I did have a cup of coffee with Natalie. Talked about this and that, and the child support. She's being really patient about that.

"Got myself online banking and a computer. Any minute of the day or night, I can see just how deep in the hole I am."

"Coffee with Natalie?" Gunny said, turning the conversation back to Jamaal's real news. "Now how did that go."

"Like I said, she was cool. I'm doing the best I can with the child support and arrears and she's okay with it," Jamaal said. "Hey, you know, somethin's better than nothing."

"Sounds promising. Overall, how do things stand now?" Gunny asked.

"Honestly, could be worse," Jamaal said. "I got my part-time work at the parts store and that's helping me knock down some bills and build up my savings. Next baby step—ain't such a baby anymore—looking for one thousand dollars in savings.

"Talked to the personnel department at the packing plant about getting some training. Nice lady—Melinda Clark—she said there were some possibilities and also asked if I'd be interested in work with the logistics team—shipping and receiving. You know I said yes to that."

Gunny sat down in the rocking chair on the porch. Jamaal sat on the porch swing.

"First time I totaled up my debts, it was more than fifteen thousand," Jamaal said. "Just this last week, I got it under ten thousand."

"Damn," Gunny said. "That's good work, son. And you got close to a thousand in savings?"

"Oh, yeah," Jamaal said. "That too."

"That war—that battle you're fighting," Gunny said. "If I'm not mistaken, I believe you have established a pretty strong position and you are taking the initiative. You ain't just hunkering down, taking enemy fire. You are on the offensive."

"Well, yeah, maybe," Jamaal said. "But I'll tell you right now, I am tired and hungry. Where is that old man with our dinner?"

"Zeke?" Gunny said. "He'll be right along. Probably stopped off at the bakery for some serious dessert. He may run a little late once in a while, but that's one man you can always count on, Jamaal. You go into a battle with him, he won't ever let you down."

Rule Number 7

"So, are we going to meet the big man today?" Jamaal was seated on a city bus next to the Rev. The old man took the window seat.

"We're up to rule number seven," Jamaal continued. "This my lucky day? Get to meet the richest man in New Babylon? Some big time company president or CEO?"

"A lucky number," the Rev said. "Appropriate. Very appropriate. But to answer your question, no, not a CEO. We're going to meet someone in a different line of work—more like investing and insurance."

The downtown bus they were on traveled to a very different part of the city. Jamaal recognized several landmarks—they were close to the edge of his old neighborhood.

When the Rev signaled the bus driver, they exited on a corner not three blocks from where Pink had robbed the Q-Mart.

He wondered where Pink was incarcerated. Prison was a scary place. If Pink was in there, that would make it worse.

"You have friends around here?" Jamaal said to the Rev.

"More of an acquaintance," the Rev said. "Met him while I was helping arrange a truce in a gang war. A man to respect."

Jamaal had been staying away from this part of town. At first, he was just letting things cool down, but now, he just liked it better around Pacific Avenue.

The Rev headed for a doorway next to a storefront. No signs—not even a bell or buzzer. They walked up a flight of stairs and as they reached the landing, the door opened. A very large man wearing a suit with a large bulge in the area where you might wear a shoulder holster was facing them.

"We are expected," the Rev said.

The man nodded and showed them into a waiting room. The walls were black. Several black wooden chairs lined one wall. Nobody else was waiting. The big man opened the second door, disappeared briefly, then stepped out and gestured to the Rev and Jamaal to enter.

The walls of the dimly lit office were black. The only white light came from a desk lamp and a computer screen on a desk that stood almost in the center of the room. A purplish glow illuminated a large—make that huge— aquarium on one side of the room.

Jamaal recognized the man dressed entirely in black who was standing next to the aquarium.

"Booker," he whispered to the Rev. "Lennie Booker? 'No Limit' Lennie Booker? You know him?"

"Mr. Booker and I have been acquainted for a while," the Rev said in his normal voice. "How long now? Back about ten years?"

"'Bout that," Booker said as he leaned over a small fish bowl near the aquarium. Jamaal saw him catch a live gold-fish in a small net. He opened the cover of the aquarium, and dropped the goldfish into the big tank. It started swimming around, and suddenly, it disappeared. A big blue-greenish fish had snapped it down in one gulp.

"Big fish eat little fish," Booker said, putting the net down.

"Piranha," he said. "Snack time. Supper is more sub-stantial. Big fish can eat big fish, too. But you're not here for fish stories."

"No, sir, Mr. Booker," Jamaal said. "The Rev, he said I was going to meet an investment and insurance advisor."

Booker laughed. "Sounds almost respectable."

"Wait a minute now," Jamaal said. "You? You're the richest man in town?"

Booker laughed again.

"I'm a reasonably successful entrepreneur," Booker said. "But I'm not up there with the big-time attorneys and doctors. And some of my colleagues who specialize in the pharmaceutical industry—they likely do much more business than me. Bigger risk. Bigger reward. Which leads us right to the subject for our meeting."

"Investments and insurance," the Rev said.

"Investments and insurance," Booker said. "Your name again?"

"Jamaal. Jamaal Thomas."

"Well, Jamaal, you know me by reputation if not personally," Booker said.

"Yes sir. Gambling. You want to place a bet—on anything—you talk to one of Mr. Booker's friends," Jamaal said. "Win, you get paid quick. Lose, you better pay up quick. If you do any other business, any 'pharmaceuticals,' like you said, or any other kind of business, you don't mess with Mr. Booker and he don't mess with you."

"Got all that about right," Booker said. "Now the thing about my business of course, is that it's all 'off the books.' Suits and cops they might say it's all 'illegal.' So that means there are folks I got to pay, so they go look for some other entrepreneur to hassle."

"Okay," Jamaal said. "I understand, but what's all that that got to do with investing and insurance?"

"Everything," Booker said.

Jamaal stared at the man in black. Booker remained silent.

"I'm not getting this," Jamaal said.

"Here's your rule, Jamaal," the Rev said. "Surprised the heck out of me when Mr. Booker explained it to me. Get your notebook. Write this down."

Booker watched Jamaal prepare to take notes, then proceeded.

"Investing and insurance are nothin' but high-toned, fancy ass ways to gamble. It's just all about knowing the odds," Booker said.

"That's it. Investing and insurance: legal ways to gamble. You understand that and you know everything you need to know about stocks and bonds and mutual funds and term insurance and whole life and all that crap," Booker said.

"It's all the same damn thing I do. It's upscale, sure, but it's all just fancy bookmaking."

"Now, wait a minute," Jamaal said.

"Hear him out," the Rev said.

"It's like this," Booker said, "you buy a stock in a company, you're placing a bet. You hope its price is gonna go up, pay off and make you a winner. Maybe pay you a little dividend, too, kinda like earning some interest.

"But maybe the company falls apart. Stock goes down. No dividends. You lose.

"Big, well-known companies—they may be better bets—less risky. Probably won't tank. But they may not have a big payoff either.

"Some brand-new company you never heard of—place your bet there—you may get a real big payoff," Booker said. "But it's more risky. Better chance it goes belly-up and you gonna lose everything.

"Mutual funds—you heard of them?" Booker said.

"Yeah," Jamaal said.

"Okay, that's the same thing. Only instead of betting one stock, you bet on a whole bunch of companies that some smart people—portfolio managers they call 'em—have picked. You're playing the field—like betting the pari-mutuel. One stock breaks down it won't be so bad. Less risky. But if one goes great, the rest stay the same, then there's less reward.

"Lot of the smart money gets bet on 'index' funds," Booker continued. "An index fund has all the stocks from something like the Dow Jones index or the S&P 500 index in it. You buy an index fund, you're betting on the whole damn bunch of them.

"With all these bets, you gotta find out what the hidden cost is. That's like the vig you pay your friendly neighborhood loan shark. Only with mutual funds and index funds they call it a 'load.'

"If you gonna be street wise—make that Wall Street-wise—you look for a 'no-load' fund. The 'load' is the fees they charge you. Any time you buy any of this stuff, you ask about how much it costs—everything—all the costs.

"Insurance," Booker said. He was on a roll. "Now for me, I make my regular payments to a few, carefully selected members of our law enforcement community. Odds are real good that these small contributions to the welfare of the men in blue will significantly reduce the possibility of unforeseen business interruptions.

"Same principle applies in any other kind of insurance," he continued. "Take life insurance. Works the same way. Insurance premium—the payments you make—that's just another kind of bet. You're betting with the insurance company on whether you gonna die.

"Car insurance? What're the odds you gonna crack up your ride?

"You get under the hood—look at what drives all this stuff—it's just figuring out the odds and placing bets. You follow?"

"Yeah," Jamaal said. "Mostly."

"Now, two more important things you gotta understand," Booker said.

"First, just like when you're gambling, remember this: The house always wins. You write that down."

Jamaal nodded. He started writing.

"Wha'd I say?" Booker demanded.

"The house always wins," Jamaal said.

"That's right. You remember that. The house *always* wins," Booker said.

"Casino owner, stockbroker, insurance agent, state lottery, financial advisor, me—your friendly neighborhood bookie—in the long run, we will always come out ahead," Booker said.

"We set the odds. We're in business to make money. We are not dummies, so … the house is always going to win.

"That means if you gonna be smart about your investing and insurance, you got to know the odds *and* you gotta figure out just *how much* the house is gonna win.

"What are the odds? How risky is the proposition? Can you lose everything you bet? What's it gonna cost you to place your bet? What's the rake or the vig—is some sales rep getting a fee or maybe a percentage of your action? Somebody sells you something—some fund or insurance or anything—how's he gonna get paid? Gotta be gettin' something, right? Gotta make a living? You gotta dig and find out how much it costs because …?"

Booker paused. He waited for Jamaal to come up with the answer.

"The house always wins?" Jamaal finally said.

"That's right," Booker said. "The house always wins."

"The other big thing you gotta remember," Booker continued. "If it sounds too good to be true, it is."

"If it sounds too good to be true, it is," Jamaal repeated as he made more notes.

"If you was gambling—you'd call it a sucker bet. Someone offers you a proposition that is just an obvious, no brainer, sure thing. What happens if you take that bet?"

Booker paused and waited until Jamaal looked up at him. And he kept waiting.

"You lose?" Jamaal said.

"You lose," Booker said.

"Man says to you, 'invest $5,000 with me and with increased value and compound interest, it'll be worth $10,000 in 10 years.' That sound reasonable?"

"I'd have to know more, but that sounds like it could happen," Jamaal said. "Could be a good deal."

Same dude says, 'give me five large and with my inside track and little tip I got, I'm going to get you $10,000 in ten weeks. Ten weeks. Now that really sounds sweet, right?"

"Yeah, real good," Jamaal said.

"Too good?" Booker said.

"Ahh, yeah. Too good. Too good to be true," Jamaal said. "I'd be saying goodbye to $5,000."

"You're catching on," Booker said. "You got any idea how hard it is to win if you're playing poker? A dollar or two here and there—maybe if you're real good and you're lucky you can come out far enough ahead and make a living."

"Yeah," Jamaal said.

"You really got to know the game and study the cards. Gotta know what happens to the odds every time you see a new card. Gotta know a lot of stuff—and then—you gotta be lucky.

"Investing and insurance and all that—it's all the same. You can play it safe. Find safe bets—fairly low risk places to put your money. You won't double it in ten weeks, but you won't lose it all either. But if you gonna make big bets—you got to know a lot of stuff—study it day and night and maybe get lucky.

"That's it," Booker said.

He stood up, went over to the goldfish bowl and scooped up another little fish, and opened the cover of the big aquarium.

"How much you gonna bet depends on how much you can win and how much you can afford to lose," Booker said. "Risk and reward."

Booker dropped the little fish into the tank and the waiting piranha snapped it up.

"Get it?" Booker said, turning toward Jamaal.

"Got it," Jamaal said.

THE RULES

1. PAY YOURSELF FIRST

2. IF YOU WANT TO HAVE MORE MONEY—
   SPEND LESS

3. TEENY TINY BABY STEPS
   KISS

4. NEVER PAY INTEREST
   ALWAYS <u>EARN</u> INTEREST

5. PRACTICE! PRACTICE! PRACTICE!
   GET A LITTLE BIT BETTER EVERY DAY

6. MAKE IT AUTOMATIC

7. INVESTING AND INSURANCE =
   LEGAL GAMBLING
   KNOW THE ODDS — AND REMEMBER—
   THE HOUSE ALWAYS WINS

More Trouble Ahead

Another letter that he had to go to the post office and sign for: Jamaal knew it was not good news. This time, he was being contacted by the Internal Revenue Service—the IRS. Something about not filing a tax return. Well damn, Jamaal thought. I only filed one tax return before and then I was locked up in prison and wasn't earning any money and how was I supposed to file a tax return anyhow? Damn."

Jamaal sat in a cheap plastic chair in the front part of Max Tax Back, Inc., the new occupant of a previously vacant storefront on High Street. *Many Happy Returns*—that's what one sign in the window said.

Jamaal didn't know Max Boykens, the guy who ran the place, but a bunch of people from the packing house had gone there and said he was real smart and got them money back.

Boykens was some kind of entrepreneur. First of the year, he'd start up his tax business. Seemed to have a different name every year, but in the same neighborhood. Then he'd shift over to insurance and personal financial stuff. Toward the end of the year he was advertising immigration services. He had a lot of irons in the fire.

It was convenient, Jamaal thought. Might as well start here. And don't sign anything, he reminded himself.

There were five desks in the back of the place. There were two couples getting returns done, two guys—one Jamaal recognized from the plant, and a really old lady with her daughter or guardian, who was just getting up to leave. Jamaal was next.

"Hey there," the middle aged, balding black man said, sticking out his hand. "Max Boykens, expert authority in all matters related to the IRS at your service. "You filled out our information sheet I see," he said, taking the clipboard with the form on it from Jamaal.

"Jamaal," he said. "Jamaal Thomas. Maple Avenue area. I know it well. C'mon back here, Jamaal," he said, ushering him back to the farthest and biggest desk. "Let's see how we can help you out."

Jamaal showed him his notice and described his situation. Boykens made a copy of the letter from the IRS and took notes. He listened intently and furrowed his brow. When Jamaal finished explaining about how he'd only filed one tax return, Boykens sat, deep in thought for maybe a minute. Then he made some more notes.

"Jamaal," he said finally, "I think we are going to be able to help you out.

"Now I'm going to need you to gather up some additional documentation. I will need your Social Security number and your daughter's—that child support business will come into play. If you have her mother's social—that will help.

"Now I know you haven't filed for this year, as this letter shows, but you are in the system. If you have a copy of your old tax return, that will tell us a lot. And even if you can't find the return—having those Social Security numbers will be very helpful.

"I'll put together a file for you, here. When you come back with the rest of your documentation, one of my agents will go through everything with you. We're going to look into several possibilities here, and I believe we are going to be able to take care of any worries you have with the IRS and—here's some excellent news—we're going to get you a tax refund.

"Can't say it will be thousands," Boykens continued. He was smooth. "But hundreds—likely—several hundred dollars.

"Now let's get you signed up with our client form—gives us permission to represent you in these matters."

He pushed a blank form and pen over to Jamaal.

"Just sign at the bottom there," Boykens said. "We'll fill in the rest of the information and date it."

Don't sign anything, that's what Jamaal had been thinking when he walked in the door. But here ... here was a real opportunity.

Jamaal had walked in with a big problem—letter from the IRS—hadn't filed a return. Now he was hearing that he could get several hundred dollars back from the government?

"If it sounds too good to be true ..." That was the next thought that went through Jamaal's mind. If it sounds too good to be true, it usually is.

"This meeting has been very helpful, Mr. Boykens." Jamaal picked up the pen, put it down in the middle of the form and pushed it away a few inches. "I'll have to think about this for a while."

Boykens was surprised, but recovered quickly.

"Now, Jamaal, we are heading right into our busy season," he said. "We can fit you in now—get all this resolved for you. Get it off your mind."

"Yes, sir, I appreciate that," Jamaal said. He thanked Boykens again, stood up, and headed for the door.

"If it sounds too good to be true ... " The bookmaker's words echoed in Jamaal's mind. "Definitely too good to be true," he said to himself.

The Richest Man in New Babylon

Rule Number 8

The Rev had introduced Jamaal to a lot of different people but this was about as uncomfortable as Jamaal had ever felt. He was standing on the front porch of the Grayson Funeral Home.

When they walked through the front door, everything was dark, somber and sort of—well—dead. But only for a minute.

Then the hallway, the whole first floor, echoed with cheerful laughter. A big, booming laugh from some-where—someone—who was very amused about some-thing.

"Ah," the Rev said, "he's here. Robbie. Robbie Grayson. He said he'd be expecting us."

They followed the laughter down the hallway toward the back of the building. A trim black man was sitting qui-etly behind a desk, listening to someone on the telephone. He wore a three-piece suit with the jacket hanging on the back of his office chair. He looked much too small to have had such a big laugh, but then it started again—a rolling chuckle that grew into a full belly laugh.

"Go on, man, go on," he said. "Don't think I'll believe that story for a second, even if you swear it's true. But I gotta go now, got the Rev and a young man he wants me to meet are standing right here in the office."

After a little more back and forth and a few more chuckles, Robbie Grayson finished his call and greeted the Rev and Jamaal.

Robbie Grayson was about the same age as the Rev, an "old guy" Jamaal thought. The Rev was short, but this dude was shorter. He was fit; looked good in his suit.

He gestured them over to a small seating area in the cor-ner of his office.

"This will have to be a little on the short side," he was saying. "I have a family coming in at three to make arrangements. I can't keep them waiting."

"No problem," the Rev said. "Jamaal is a quick study."

The funeral director turned toward Jamaal.

"I'm guessing you're surprised to be here," he said.

"Don't much care for funerals," Jamaal said. "Been to some—friends, my age, and … well, I just don't care much for funerals."

"That can be hard, man goes before his time," Grayson said. "Takes a while to heal."

"Over the years you may learn to see the experience a little differently," Grayson said. "A funeral can also be a warm, emotional, social gathering—a celebration—a send-off for the star and a kind of party for the rest of us."

"Well, I guess …" Jamaal started.

"Don't worry about it now," Grayson said. "Takes time. But as much as we seem to be concerned with death and dying around here, we're working to serve the living. And in helping the people who come in here to plan for a funeral, we've learned a lot about what it takes to take care of the living. Reverend Wright wants me to share some of that experience with you."

"Robbie deals with life and death matters," the Rev said. "Got your notebook?"

Jamaal already had it opened and waited, pen in hand.

"The big thing—the 'rule' that I can share with you is this," Grayson said. "Things never stay 'the same.' We are always either growing or dying, getting better or getting worse, becoming richer or growing poorer.

"It's human nature to think that everything is just the same today as it was yesterday. But it's not. Everything is constantly changing. May not be much. You may not notice. But there's no such thing as things being 'the same.'"

"I understand what you're saying," Jamaal said. "At least I get the general idea, anyway. But why does that matter?"

"A good question," said the Rev. "Why indeed, Robbie?"

"Several reasons," Grayson said.

"First, for people having hard times, dealing with financial difficulty, emotional troubles, loss of a loved one—it's a reminder that you won't always feel as bad as you do today. You're not stuck in this bad place. There will be change," Grayson said.

"This too shall pass," the Rev said.

"Exactly," Grayson said. Then he continued.

"Second, for people who are in a good place, it's a reminder to be grateful for what you have and to keep working on the little things that will make life better for you. If you're not making progress toward your goals, then you're falling back. You gotta keep moving forward," Grayson said.

"And another thing I think of a lot—because of my profession—you need to look ahead and plan for the future."

"You mean like making financial plans—goals for your savings and such—I'm on that," Jamaal said.

"That's good, but you also need to consider the bigger picture," Grayson said. "We are none of us immortal, though it may seem that way to a strong young man such as yourself. Too many young people ignore thinking about this possibility: What will happen if I should die? It creates all kinds of troubles for the family and friends; leaves them trying to guess what a person would want and leaves important decisions up to state laws.

"All sorts of problems can occur. It can get ugly," Grayson continued. "And all the problems can be avoided if you keep your eyes wide open and plan ahead."

"That's not a problem for me," Jamaal said. "I don't have nothing worth fighting over."

"You might be surprised," Grayson said. "You pass, that will terminate a lot of debts. Any savings may well be transferable to your heirs. But there are costs associated with passing—that is my business after all—so how is that going to be handled?

"You may have insurance from work or elsewhere. How will that be distributed? In an accidental death, there may be some compensation—could be a sizable sum—how will that be handled? Who do you trust to help you deal with these issues?

"And there's more. Are you willing to be an organ donor? You have any charities you want to support? If you are severely injured and on life support do you want 'every effort' made to keep your body alive—even if your mind is gone?"

"Man, I don't *want* to think about that stuff," Jamaal said.

"I don't know anyone who really wants to think about the possibility of dying," Grayson said. "But, if you are going to be a grown up, responsible person, it is something you have to do. Otherwise you are placing the burden on others and taking the chance that your own last wishes will not be fulfilled."

"But it's … it is so hard," Jamaal said.

"Life-and-death matters," Grayson said.

"I don't know," Jamaal said.

"What about that rule I shared with you?" Grayson said. "What did you write down?"

"Things never stay 'the same,'" Jamaal said. "Things are always changing—getting better or getting worse. I'm workin' on moving in the 'better' direction."

"You're taking responsibility," Grayson said. "Doing things right. It's important to plan for a solid financial future. It's also important to make provisions—just in case."

"So, I need to have a will?" Jamaal said.

"Yes, you do. A will and another document that's called a 'living will.' You can get started with this online, too. Won't cost you too much. As you get older and have more responsibilities," you're going to need to keep it updated," Grayson said. "It'll be time to talk to an attorney. Have someone who really understands the law and your personal situation."

"I don't know …" Jamaal said.

"Oh, you know," Grayson said. "You know what you need to do now. And you are in a great place to do it. You are young, strong and working hard to build a great future for yourself. You're growing—not dying. All this planning is 'just in case.'

"You can do this," Grayson said.

"I guess," Jamaal replied. "Yeah, I guess."

THE RULES

1. PAY YOURSELF FIRST

2. IF YOU WANT TO HAVE MORE MONEY—
   SPEND LESS

3. TEENY TINY BABY STEPS
   KISS

4. NEVER PAY INTEREST
   ALWAYS EARN INTEREST

5. PRACTICE! PRACTICE! PRACTICE!
   GET A LITTLE BIT BETTER EVERY DAY

6. MAKE IT AUTOMATIC

7. INVESTING AND INSURANCE =
   LEGAL GAMBLING
   KNOW THE ODDS — AND REMEMBER—
   THE HOUSE ALWAYS WINS

8. THINGS NEVER STAY 'THE SAME'

Finding Resolution

The letter from the IRS still weighed on Jamaal's mind. You get one letter, Jamaal thought, pretty soon you'll get another. And soon after that, you're going to be in some kind of trouble.

Okay. Got to figure this out, Jamaal thought. Where to start?

"Damn," Jamaal said out loud to himself. He even gave himself a dope slap. He shook his head, marveling at his own stupidity. Jamaal grabbed his notebook, walked out the door and headed for the Pacific Avenue Branch Library.

Mrs. Ross checked him in for computer time. "Workstation number seven," she said. It was a little out of the way, tucked in a corner. Jamaal liked it. She recommended that he start with the IRS.gov website, and soon Jamaal was finding answers to most of his questions. For one thing, he learned, there was no legal requirement to file a tax return if you didn't owe any taxes.

That's a relief, Jamaal thought. But even so, why did I get that letter?

Mrs. Ross came to where Jamaal was working. She had several books and a suggestion.

"The IRS has a special program—Volunteer Income Tax Assistance—everyone refers to it as VITA. Volunteers, some of them with a lot of experience, help people with their taxes. A lot of seniors come in. It's very popular," she said.

"Well, I'm not sure whether I actually have to file a return," Jamaal said. "I'm still trying to figure out why I got this letter."

"One of the VITA volunteers, Ben Israel, runs the program," Mrs. Ross said. "Maybe he'd be willing to help you out. He's a very nice man. A mensch."

"A mensch?" Jamaal said.

"It's a Yiddish word. Look it up," she said, spelling it out for him. "We keep in touch by e-mail, so I have his address. If you're interested, I could send him a message with your contact information."

"Well, sure," Jamaal said. "I'm still using that e-mail address you helped me set up."

He wrote out his e-mail address on a slip of paper and gave it to Mrs. Ross.

"You can tell him I'm digging in on the IRS website, but I would really appreciate it if an expert could help me confirm what I think I know."

Two days later, Ben Israel and Jamaal met in one of the library's quiet study rooms.

A mensch, it turned out was a "decent and responsible person," and "a person of integrity and honor" and "someone to admire and emulate with a strong sense of right and wrong." As soon as he met Mr. Israel, Jamaal knew Mrs. Ross was right.

Mr. Israel was short, thin and almost entirely bald. And he was an old guy—almost as old as Miss Booth, Jamaal thought. And he seemed just as sharp. He was a retired certified public accountant, so he knew a lot about taxes. He was really funny, too

"Your assumption about last year is correct," Mr. Israel said, after listening to Jamaal's description of his situation and his take on it. "You don't need to file a return for last year—the year you spent mostly in prison. The 'state pay' that you describe isn't going to put you in a taxable income bracket. Did you have any additional earnings during that calendar year?"

"Well, like I said, I worked 'off the books' for a guy—a little delivery and collection work ..."

"No W2s involved?" Israel said. "No 1099s?"

"You mean any kind of official forms or money getting reported? Nah, the way that kind of business is conducted, it's strictly cash."

"Now, what you need to focus on is what you are going to do going forward," Israel said. "With your work at the meat packing house and the auto parts store, all of that is being reported?"

"Yes, sir," Jamaal said. "But I am still doing odd jobs—snow shoveling and stuff like that. So I get little bits of money—mostly cash—from a bunch of people."

"Okay. Now if you really want to handle this correctly—live up to the letter of the law—you need to keep records for all that income. Amount earned, who paid you, when you received the payment—that sort of thing.

"Now the letter from the IRS," Israel continued. "We can't be positive but—is it possible that you earned more than $600 from some company?" Israel asked. "Any time a company pays someone $600 or more, the company is required to send the individual and the IRS information about it. That information is generally referred to as a '1099.' Any chance someone sent you a 1099 last year?"

"No, sir," Jamaal said.

"Okay," Mr. Israel said. "Going forward, here are a couple of things to be careful about," Mr. Israel continued. "That $600 figure isn't written in stone anywhere. Tax laws change. When you're an independent businessman, you have to pay attention to them and the changes that affect you.

"Also, there's always the possibility that the IRS received a 1099 from someone, but you didn't—so you don't know that the income was reported. Whenever you receive pay from a reputable company, it should keep track of how much you have earned and send you and the IRS 1099 forms. Keep that in mind when tax time comes around."

"And what about that letter I got?" Jamaal said.

"Probably something the computer system at the IRS created automatically. The systems there are highly automated, especially for dealing with simple tax returns.

"The letter has instructions on it," Mr. Israel said. "Based on what you said, you don't have anything to worry about. Follow the instructions and call the IRS."

"What?" Jamaal said. "Talk to the IRS?"

"Why not?" Israel said. "There are some terrific people who work for the IRS. Very helpful to tax professionals—like I was. They can be a great help when assisting people with tax concerns like you."

"But all you ever hear about them …"

"The agency has suffered from a lot of bad press," Israel said. "You want a great country? Great parks? Great schools? Great roads? You have to pay for it. All I ask for is that it be fair—everybody pay a fair share. The people who work at the Internal Revenue Service are hardworking public servants and they try to make that happen."

"Talk to the IRS?" Jamaal said.

"They can be very helpful," Israel said.

"And now, for you, going forward, you have some challenges," Israel said. "Since you have two primary employers, plus the odds and ends of work you are picking up, you need to keep careful records.

"As I told you before, log all your extra income, the source, the amount and date. When you have business expenses, keep track of them, too. It may not be important to you right now, but these are good habits to develop as you get more successful and have more income.

"And, in your investigations on IRS.gov, make sure you learn about the Earned Income Tax Credit—the EITC," Israel said. "Based on what you told me, I think that might come into effect for you when you file your tax return for this year."

"EITC," Jamaal repeated, writing in his notebook.

"When tax time comes around—starting about the end of January next year, come see me," Israel said. "We'll be setting up our VITA program again here in the library."

"Yes, sir, Mr. Israel. Yes, sir."

"I'm an old man, so the 'sir'—a little respect—I can live with that. But please, just call me Ben."

Jamaal smiled and shook the older man's hand.

"Thank you, Ben."

More Coffee and More

"Now, this part basically says that anything I got—in case I die—will go to Jameela. And over here," Jamaal said, pointing to another part of the document, "that specifies that until she is either twenty-one years old or she graduates from college, that you, as her mom, will control any assets."

Nearly empty coffee cups bracketed two stacks of paperwork.

"Right now, my estate is nothing," Jamaal said. "I owe more than I got. That's changing, but for now, there are no assets.

"But here," he said, moving to the other pile of paperwork, "is an insurance policy. Not much, only fifty thousand dollars, but it is something and … well … it's a start. Also, I got some insurance through my job at the packing plant—that would be included in an estate, and if there was any accidental death benefit or anything, that would in there, too.

"I mean, I know it ain't all that much. Drop in the bucket. But I thought you should know so that, just in case, you know, you can be prepared. Just trying to plan ahead a little bit. You know …"

Jamaal was running out of words.

Natalie just sat there, across the booth from him. Jamaal couldn't tell exactly what she was thinking, except that she wasn't mad at him, he knew that for sure.

"Jamaal," she said, finally breaking a long silence. "Jamaal, dammed if I don't think you are growing up."

Sunday Dinner—Summer

The usual suspects—Jamaal, the Rev and Gunny—gathered around the grill in Gunny's back yard to admire dinner. These men were carnivores. The objects of their admiration were three thick, beautifully marbled, USDA prime steaks.

"Not what you find in the supermarket," Jamaal said, as he prepared them for grilling with salt and pepper. Jamaal had insisted on bringing the main course this evening.

"Mr. Markowsky over at the butcher shop, he set these aside for us last week," Jamaal said. "A little aging, he told me, would help concentrate the flavor."

Gunny was still making a few adjustments with the grill. "Steak that fine, nothin' but searing over an open flame will do," he had said. Now he was spreading the bed of charcoal, adding some wood chips and fanning the coals to get the grill 'just right' for the main course. Plates and utensils, side dishes and condiments were ready and waiting on the dining room table.

"We will not have this fine dinner disrupted by the arrival or any gnats or mosquitoes," the Rev had said, expressing his preference for indoor seating.

Gunny raked the coals, then got everything red hot using a fan. "Give it a minute now to settle down, give the grate a scrape and a little oil, and we are ready to go," he said.

The high heat of the August afternoon had faded. Humidity was low. The yard was exceptionally pleasant. The

Rev was right though—another ten or twenty minutes and the bugs would begin to arrive.

"Yo. How are things going?" Gunny asked as they stood back, waiting for the precise right moment to put the steaks on the heat.

"It's scary," Jamaal said. "Scary good. I'm getting more hours at the parts store—worked six hours today. I got assigned to the logistics department at the packing house. Getting a little more money and learning a lot about shipping, receiving and scheduling."

It was time. Jamaal put the steaks on.

"Number of big debts I still have, I've cut that in half and the total, it's way less than half—more like a third from where I started.

"What happened? How'd you get this far so fast?" Gunny said. "Did you get lucky? Win the lottery or something?"

"Aw, c'mon, Gunny, you know I been working my backside off."

"Of course, you have," Gunny said. "And all the good stuff that's happening—maybe it's on account of you having a good plan based on the rules we keep throwing at you? That and you busting your butt."

He pointed at the grill.

"Might want to be thinking about turning those steaks," he said. "At least one for me—I put my order in for rare."

Jamaal turned the steaks. They looked great.

"You getting along okay with Natalie?" the Rev asked.

"Yeah," Jamaal said. "Yeah, that part is scary good, too. And I'm spending time with Jameela.

"I made out a will—Rev knows about that 'cause he's my executor—and I bought an insurance policy. Went over all that with Natalie and she sounded ... well ... she sounded impressed.

"Y'know, Gunny, you kept telling me that I was 'going to war' and 'fighting battles', and you were right, at least for a while. But now ..."

"Doesn't feel quite the same?" Gunny said. "Maybe that's on account of you're winning?"

"Jamaal, pay attention to the steaks," the Rev said. "I'm thinking it's just about time ..."

"You're right, old man," Jamaal said. "It's about time. Let's eat."

It Takes a Man

Plant maintenance staff left work a little ahead of the main shift change. Jamaal was out the front door and starting to cross the street when the big, maroon Mercedes pulled in front on him.

The dark-tinted passenger window rolled down. Jamaal didn't see a face, but he heard Doughboy's voice.

"Get in."

The passenger door swung open.

Jamaal stared into the dark interior of the car. Nothing.

"Get in."

The voice was agitated. Angry. Insistent.

Jamaal stood still. Frozen.

"Get in. Get in, or one of the boys up front are gonna shoot you down like some poor dumb mother what got in the middle of my business and was too damn stupid to get out the way in time."

Jamaal got in.

"Close the damn door," Doughboy said.

Jamaal pulled the door shut, the window slid up and the big machine purred into motion. Doughboy was alone in the back seat with Jamaal. A guy with a street name like Stick or something—Jamaal knew him vaguely—was driving. The other guy, riding shotgun, Jamaal didn't know him. But he was a scary dude—hard timer, you could tell. Doughboy had upgraded his enforcement division bigtime.

They cruised a while, heading back toward High Street as best Jamaal could tell, looking through the deeply tinted windows.

Doughboy didn't say anything for a long time. Long, long time. Jamaal decided he was going to wait him out. Hell, Doughboy was giving him a ride halfway to Pacific

Avenue. Jamaal was going to the library, anyway. Save him a hike or the bus fare.

"I got a little job that needs to get done and you're gonna do it," Doughboy finally said.

"A job?" Jamaal said. "Hey, maybe you don't know it, but I got a job." He shook his head. "Man, I got like three jobs, sometimes four. I don't need another job."

"Listen up, Jamaal," Doughboy started. "This here is a one-time thing. A little driving, meet a guy, do some shopping, turn around and come home, that's it. No biggie. Just need a nice fresh face—sweet little boy scout like yourself. You can handle this, no problem."

"Man, I got responsibilities … " Jamaal started.

Doughboy cut him off. "You got responsibilities? You got responsibilities! Man, I got a ton more than that. I got a damn war on my hands," Doughboy said. "I got some Latino creeps moving in on the south side. Got no morals. No damn honor. Shoot you soon as look at you.

"And I got Russians movin' in, too. And they're even worse. Seems like they're taking over distribution from the Mexicans. Still supplying the gangs, but they want to eliminate any mid-level competition—and I been handling some of that. I got people gettin' killed.

"So, if you think you got responsibilities bigger than my responsibilities, then you tell me that getting your crew bloody and gettin' some of 'em dead ain't just a little more 'responsible.'"

Doughboy was shaking. Anger. Frustration. Ready to boil over.

Jamaal was silent. He felt the big vehicle slow and stop.

"Listen, I got this little job," Doughboy said. "Need a reliable man to take a drive out of state. Got a man lined up who's gonna purchase a few serious weapons and ammo. We gotta be able to defend ourselves. These new guys—they comin' in with heavy artillery. Street guns ain't gonna cut it."

Jamaal heard something more in Doughboy's voice. He wasn't sure, but maybe it was fear.

"Are you gonna take care of this for me?" Doughboy said.

"Man, I …" Jamaal started, "I still ain't got a license.

"Yeah, I expected that line," Doughboy said. "That's why I got a license, credit card, company ID, insurance papers—got them all lined up. Got you a different name and a good social—they'll all run clean. We get a picture of your handsome face—you won't have any problems with license and ID."

Jamaal felt trapped there inside the cabin of the big car with three men. The Mercedes had been parked on on High Street for a while now.

"Damn, I gotta talk to you in private," Jamaal said, lowering his voice. He yanked on the door handle. It kind of surprised him when the door actually opened.

"In private!" Jamaal said, when he saw the two front doors start to open.

Doughboy got out of the back seat on the street side of the car. He cupped his hand and gave the enforcer some quiet instructions. The scary dude and the driver got back in the car and closed their doors.

Jamaal walked away from the car, toward a tall chain-link fence that surrounded a vacant lot. This was close to the same place where he had been arrested. Just a little further up—closer to the corner. He was trying to remember if the chain link fence had been there back then.

"You can take care of this in a weekend," Doughboy said. "Need to do it on a weekend—next week. There's this big gun show. You can buy damn near anything and there's hardly any checks. It's like a big weapons supermarket."

"Dontrelle," Jamaal said.

Doughboy turned his head sharply to look at Jamaal.

"Dontrelle Williams," Jamaal continued. "That's your name. Dontrelle Williams, the kid I met in third grade. Dontrelle—my best friend for—what was it—three or four years—until my mama got so bad and I got put in social services."

Doughboy was just standing, staring at Jamaal.

"Remember how we used to play with those little plastic blocks? You liked the spaceships and astronauts the best. Me, I was all in for cars and motorcycles and stuff with gears and motors. And when you got that video game console, Dontrelle. That was so cool. We worked our way through all the levels. We were a great team back then."

Doughboy—Dontrelle—had turned away from Jamaal. He was looking toward the big Mercedes.

Jamaal went up behind him now and put a hand on his shoulder.

"Dontrelle," he said. "I can't do this job for you. I understand. You got some serious shit comin' down, and you gotta do what you gotta do. But I can't make this run for you. I can't do it. I won't do it."

Dontrelle ... it was Dontrelle now ... turned to face his childhood friend. He wanted to say something but wasn't finding any words.

"You tell them that I'm a coward," Jamaal said. "That I was scared. That I wet my pants at the thought of taking on this job. Tell 'em you decided I was too big a risk—that I'd screw it up."

They stood quiet, face to face for a while. Then Jamaal broke the silence.

"I gotta get going. If you need me for something I can actually help you with—or you gotta send somebody to kill me or ... or ... whatever ... I'll be at the library."

Jamaal turned and started walking, slow and calm and shaking inside, toward the corner.

"Watch your back, you chicken shit!" Doughboy was calling him out. "Damn," Doughboy continued, and Jamaal could hear car doors opening. "Damned if I know why I thought he could'a done this job. Takes a man, you know," Doughboy said. "Takes a man."

The Richest Man in New Babylon

Rule Number 9

"What happened? That's the first question anyone wants to ask. Don't be shy," the man sitting across from Jamaal said.

"Improvised explosive device—IED. Big sucker. Destroyed the truck in front of us and tore the whole bottom out of our Humvee."

Lance Corporal Amos Fredericks, USMC, retired, a black man with shoulder length locs, sat in a wheelchair to the right of Gunny at a small table in the back of the Pacific Avenue Diner. Scars marred the right side of his face. The Rev sat on his left while Jamaal sat straight across from Fredericks.

"So now I am fully equipped with two prosthetic legs, one ManuTrol bio-electronic Type GC mechanical hand, and a terrific collection of scars that border on body art," Fredericks said. "This quirky smile of mine is accompanied by about eighty percent loss of vision in my right eye."

The young veteran paused, then continued.

"And man, am I lucky."

Jamaal said nothing.

"Seriously. Lucky," Fredericks said. "Now don't you go thinking I'm stupid and think that this was all a good thing because it was not. Is not. For one thing, it hurt. It hurt a lot, and still hurts. It screwed up all my plans for the future. It's scary, you know. Get hurt, feel like ... like really, really bad, and you got no idea what's coming. Whole thing sucks."

"So, what are you doing now?" Jamaal asked.

"School, man. Going to school. Just finishing up my associate's degree and heading for State University in the fall."

"Yeah?" Jamaal said.

"Yeah. And that is something I never thought I'd be doing. I was never any kind of student," Fredericks said. "I mean I did okay in high school, but I never expected to go any further."

"And now?" Jamaal said.

"Not a hundred percent sure," Fredericks said. "Could go into computers, maybe. I've done well in classes and I'm the 'go to' guy for my family and friends. I have a business professor who said I should study accounting. I got a psychology professor who is encouraging me to get into the counseling profession.

"So, I got two things for you," he continued. "One—just a piece of advice and the other—a rule for that little notebook the Rev says you're keeping."

"Well, sure," Jamaal said. He fumbled briefly with his coat, found his notebook and opened it.

"Here's the advice," Fredericks said. "You get through a tough time—you use it. I survived getting blown up—got through it. Now I'm damn well gonna use it. You survived incarceration—you got through it. Now use it. You're tougher now, stronger. You're a survivor. Anything else comes now, it's gotta be easier than that."

"Yeah," Jamaal said. "Some ways it's easier. But when you come out with a rap sheet …"

"You got a lot more mobility than me, brother, and you're going to work through the stuff that comes with incarceration."

"Yeah, I know," Jamaal said.

"You think you know," Fredericks said. "You think, but deep down inside, you've still got a chunk of 'poor me'—of feeling sorry for yourself—inside you. You think life is unfair.

"Well it's true. What happened to you—what happened to me—it really sucks. Life isn't 'fair.' Good men get killed. Bad guys get rich. And guys like us, we got to work like hell every day just to make it to tomorrow.

"And, you know what—it's okay to feel a little sorry for yourself from time to time," Fredericks said. "It's true. But it's also true that we made it through some tough times—damn tough times. We have been tested. We survived. And once we got past that, we can get past anything."

"Okay," Jamaal said. "Advice received."

"Now the rule," Fredericks said. "I learned this one really well while I was in the hospital and in physical therapy."

"Okay," Jamaal said.

"Now, this is going to sound … well … simple minded."

"Okay," Jamaal said.

"Stupid maybe," Fredericks said. "But trust me, it's true."

"I'm listening," Jamaal said.

"The most important things in life are free," Fredericks said. "You can write that down. The most important things in life are free."

Jamaal wasn't writing. He was looking at Fredericks. The man in the wheelchair held onto him with his one good eye. He locked in on Jamaal. He spoke again.

"I know you're worried about money and being in debt and all that," Fredericks said. "And it's important, that's for sure. But it's not the *most* important part of your life. There are times when you have to push all your day-to-day worries aside and see the big picture.

"Think about—say taking a walk—around the block. Don't cost nothing," Fredericks said. "Now get your legs blown off, you understand how important some things are.

"You been to the ocean—take a walk on the beach—since you got out of incarceration?" Fredericks asked.

"No," Jamaal said.

"Try it, then," Fredericks said. "Remember what it felt like when you were inside, you know, in prison and all. Then take a walk on the beach. I'll bet it feels a little different. A little better.

"You got friends?" Fredericks asked.

"Not many," Jamaal said. Then he glanced at Gunny on one side and the old man next to him. "But some," he added.

"Good friends—you can't buy them with money How about your health? Feeling okay? See and hear well?"

"Fine, just fine," Jamaal said.

"Bet you can beat me in a forty-yard dash, too," Fredericks said with a little laugh.

"Maybe," Jamaal said, nodding. "Yeah, I'm pretty fortunate that way. Doing okay."

"Got family?" Fredericks asked.

"Not much," Jamaal said. "Sister. And she's been good—hangin' in with me this time round. That's been important. And I got a few aunts, uncles, and cousins, but we're not close. And I got a little girl. Jameela. She's three and a half now."

"You got a daughter?" Fredericks said. "Man, you are one lucky …" He paused. "A little girl? You got a picture?"

Jamaal was flustered. "Ah, no. Don't happen to …"

"Man, you know, you got to start paying attention to all the really important stuff around you," Fredericks said. "My sister's got a kid—little girl just about the same age as yours. She is such a—she's just so neat. You hold that child and remember—*this* is what's really important.

"Are you hearing me?" Fredericks asked. "You buying what I'm selling?"

"Like you said, sounds simple," Jamaal said. "Sounds kind of dumb, but ..."

"You're right," Fredericks said. "Simple. And dumb. An English teacher's going to say it's a cliché. But, say it back to me, just so I'm sure you know what we're talking about."

"The rule?"

"The rule," Fredericks said.

"Yeah. Okay." Jamaal started writing. "So—looks like this is rule number nine," he said. He paused a moment and looked at what he had written. "Man, this sounds so, so ... kind of sissy like."

He glanced up again at the man in the wheelchair. That man was no damn sissy.

"Rule number nine," Jamaal continued. "The most important things in life are free."

"You think hard about that now," Fredericks said. "Healthy body. Sound mind. Good family. People you love, people who love you just for who you are. None of that costs you a penny.

"You believe in God?" Fredericks asked

"Yeah, well, sort of," Jamaal said.

"I'm not very religious myself," Fredericks said, "but I know, for a lot of folks, religion is very important. And there's no price tag on faith for a believer.

"What's the weather like today?" Fredericks asked.

"Nice," Jamaal said. "Sunshine, blue sky. So nice I even noticed it a bit when I was walking over here."

"And how much did you pay for this fine weather?"

"I'm hearing you," Jamaal said. "The most important things in life are free."

"We all hear the message. But to believe it and to live it—that can be hard," Fredericks said. "You got to be pushing back against all the people selling stuff and promoting stuff in trying to convince you that you need their 'stuff.'"

"I guess I've been learning a lot about that anyway," Jamaal said. "I mean, hell, all the money I ain't got now. I ain't been buyin' a lot of anything."

"But how are you feeling about that?" Fredericks said. "You angry? Ticked off because you can't go and buy a lot of 'stuff'?"

"Maybe," Jamaal said. "Maybe a little."

"Look at your rule there," Fredericks said. "How are you going to live it? What can you do to make it part of your daily life?"

Jamaal stared at his notebook. Then he looked back up at Fredericks.

"It's so ... I don't know ... so lame sounding."

"I know," Fredericks said. "Go ahead. Say what you're thinking."

The conversation paused again.

"Count your blessings?" Jamaal said.

"You got it," Fredericks said. "Got it in one. Now practice it—think about the parts of your life that are *really* important. About what *really* matters."

"Yeah," Jamaal said. "Yeah."

"When you do that—count your blessings—write it down," Fredericks said. "Any time you're feeling sorry for yourself, you look at that list. You'll feel better."

"Count your blessings," Jamaal said, writing in his notebook. "One," he said, continuing to write. "Not incarcerated."

He paused and looked at Fredericks.

"You know, I think this is gonna take a little while," Jamaal said.

"Hope so," Fredericks said.

"I'll work on it at home," Jamaal said.

"Good," Fredericks said.

"And, I guess I'm going to have to put your name on this list," Jamaal said.

"Damn straight," the man sitting across the table from him said.

THE RULES

1. PAY YOURSELF FIRST

2. IF YOU WANT TO HAVE MORE MONEY—
   SPEND LESS

3. TEENY TINY BABY STEPS
   KISS

4. NEVER PAY INTEREST
   ALWAYS EARN INTEREST

5. PRACTICE! PRACTICE! PRACTICE!
   GET A LITTLE BIT BETTER EVERY DAY

6. MAKE IT AUTOMATIC

7. INVESTING AND INSURANCE =
   LEGAL GAMBLING
   KNOW THE ODDS — AND REMEMBER—
   THE HOUSE ALWAYS WINS

8. THINGS NEVER STAY 'THE SAME'

9. THE MOST IMPORTANT THINGS
   IN LIFE ARE FREE

Rule Number 10

"One year," Gunny said. "Been a full year since we first met up."

They were sitting in the front parlor in Gunny's house. Jamaal shook his head. "Seems like yesterday when I got out. But now, it's so different."

Gunny had invited Jamaal and the Rev and "a few friends" over to dinner. But when Jamaal arrived, he was the only guest.

"I asked you here early," Gunny said. "I've got one more thing to go over with you. You've been working hard. Doing good work. It's paying off."

"Just following the rules," Jamaal said.

"And it's working," Gunny said.

"Now, I got one more rule for you," Gunny continued.

Jamaal smiled and pulled out his notebook. "Go ahead," he said.

"This one is easy. But there's a lot packed into it. Best part, though, is that you are already pretty much on top of it."

"You mean investing in that IRA?" Jamaal said.

"No," Gunny said, laughing. "That was a good choice though; at least that's what I think. But this is more 'big picture.'"

"Like I said," Gunny paused, then continued, "I see that you've been working hard, following the rules and putting your life together. You've already got a good handle on this last rule."

"Okay," Jamaal said, his pen ready.

"It's all up to you," Gunny said. "That's the rule: It's all up to you.

"Taking control of your life. Success. Happiness. Getting to a place where you don't have to worry about money. It's all up to you, Jamaal.

"Now Zeke—the Rev—he's likely to get God involved in all of this. But even if everything is determined by God's will—it's your hands that are going to do the work. It's your body that's going to roll out of the sack at reveille. It's your decision to save money, live responsibly and invest in the future.

"You accept help from anywhere you find it—the good Lord, good friends, a good financial advisor. Listen, get information and help from everywhere but ..."

Gunny left the sentence hanging.

"But ..." Jamaal repeated

"End of the day—it's all up to you," Gunny said. "You're learning. There are no easy answers. You follow the rules, but sometimes the rules conflict. It's complicated. You gotta make decisions. It's up to you—you have to take personal responsibility."

Jamaal was writing in his notebook.

"Taking personal responsibility also means taking family responsibility," Gunny continued. "You gotta think about the people who are close to you and about how what you do affects them."

"I'm working on that," Jamaal said.

"Yes, you are, and I'm damn proud of you for that," Gunny said. "Now, folks are going to be arriving for dinner soon so I'm just going to give you three points to add.

"First thing—attitude is everything. If you take responsibility and act like you hate it or you're annoyed about it, everybody is going to know. Like I said—it's gonna be a battle. You're goin' to war—but go to war armed with a positive attitude. Have your mind made up—you *will* succeed. Gotta overcome an obstacle: 'can do,' that's what you say to yourself. Always think positive. You'll be happier and so will the people around you.

"And now, here's a dirty little secret. Even if you're feeling awful, you can pretend you feel okay. Somebody asks 'how you feeling?' You say, 'great,' no matter how bad you're feeling inside. You fake that positive attitude and—you know what—it becomes real. Soon, you got a real positive attitude.

"Another thing—my second point—and I'm gonna sound like Zeke here. It is more important to give than to receive.

"You find ways to help other people and it's like some kind of magic. You feel better about yourself. You feel stronger. You can handle more responsibility.

"And my last thing," Gunny continued, "another part of taking personal responsibility. Your job in life includes caring for those who are less fortunate than you.

"You got strength. You've got resources. You run into someone—say someone like you were—the day you got out of incarceration—struggling a bit. Your job is to reach out, lend a hand, share your experience.

"You got all that?"

Jamaal was writing quickly and continued for another thirty seconds. Then he stopped and looked Gunny straight in the eye.

"Gettin' it," he said. "I know I still got a ways to go, but I'm getting it."

THE RULES

1. PAY YOURSELF FIRST

2. IF YOU WANT TO HAVE MORE MONEY—
   SPEND LESS

3. TEENY TINY BABY STEPS
   KISS

4. NEVER PAY INTEREST
   ALWAYS EARN INTEREST

5. PRACTICE! PRACTICE! PRACTICE!
   GET A LITTLE BIT BETTER EVERY DAY

6. MAKE IT AUTOMATIC

7. INVESTING AND INSURANCE =
   LEGAL GAMBLING
   KNOW THE ODDS — AND REMEMBER—
   THE HOUSE ALWAYS WINS

8. THINGS NEVER STAY 'THE SAME'

9. THE MOST IMPORTANT THINGS
   IN LIFE ARE FREE

10. IT'S ALL UP TO YOU

The Richest Man in New Babylon

New Beginnings

The doorbell rang. Guests arrived. Lots of guests. The Rev was first. Jamaal greeted the old man with a warm hug. He was accompanied by Karen McDonald from the daycare center. Jamaal bowed ceremoniously. "Baby steps, sensei," he said. She laughed. He clasped her hand warmly.

Miss Booth arrived accompanied by Arnie Swann. "I have something to tell you that may *interest* you," Jamaal said as he gave her a gentle hug. She laughed.

Mae Chen and Laurence Barnes were heading up the walk. Behind them he saw Robbie Grayson, the dapper funeral director, and he was with a man walking in jerky steps with the aid of crutches.

Jamaal greeted everyone on the porch. The man with Grayson was Amos Fredericks.

"No chair?" Jamaal said.

Fredericks smiled. "Not today," he said. "I'm test driving some very fancy, high tech prosthetic legs for the VA. Latest and greatest, they say. Nice to see the world from a little higher altitude. Couple more upgrades like this and I may be ready to take you in that forty-yard dash."

They both laughed.

Fredericks' arrival distracted Jamaal. He turned to greet the last group of guests and was facing Natalie and Jameela. They were accompanied by his sister, Jennifer.

After hugging his little girl—well, not so little now—nearly four years old, he extended his hand to Natalie. She took it and drew him into a gentle hug.

It felt good, Jamaal thought. It felt so good. He could get to enjoy this sort of thing.

Jennifer put an arm around his back and escorted him back inside the house.

"Well, little brother," she said, "it appears there are some people here in New Babylon who don't think you are as much of a boneheaded, troublemaking fool as I thought you were. And I guess I'm finding myself kind of agreeing with them."

The parlor in Gunny's small house was jammed. People stood around chatting, a pleasant murmur of conversation filling the room. People sharing some simple appetizers, news of the day, all people Jamaal knew. All ages, all races, and all genders. His family. His neighbors on Pacific Avenue.

"Ten'shun," Gunny said. Not his full Marine gunnery sergeant voice, but with enough authority to hush the room.

"Dinner is served," he said.

Thirteen places were set around the dining room table—more than it was designed to seat but that didn't matter at all. Jamaal started to sit between Jameela and Miss Booth.

"Jamaal," Gunny said, standing at the head of the table. "I know a young man such as yourself always wants to sit next to a beautiful woman, but I'm going to have to ask you to pass up that opportunity at this time. You are our guest of honor tonight, young man. We have a place for you right up here."

Jamaal went up to the head of the table. He sat down between the Rev and Natalie. Guests were uncovering dishes and passing plates around and then the table grew a little quieter. Everyone looked toward Jamaal

"Grace?" the Rev said.

"Oh," Jamaal murmured. He didn't kick himself for not realizing. He didn't make a joke about it, either. A man—a man accepts responsibility. A man does the best he can, and then tries to get a little bit better every day.

Jamaal asked everyone to join hands. He led the guests in a short, humble, grace, counting his blessings around the crowded table.

Speech, Speech, Speech

Empty serving dishes clustered in the center of the big table; empty plates surrounded them. Chairs pushed back, heads were turned and nodding in animated conversations. Alone in his head for a moment, Jamaal played the observer. He enjoyed seeing all these people, gathered in his honor, so visibly enjoying themselves and the company of the other guests.

Jamaal's reverie was snapped by the sharp ringing sound of the edge of a knife on a water glass. Damn, this ain't a wedding, Jamaal thought. What's the Rev doing that for?

While it was the old man who brought quiet to the happy, well-fed table, it was Gunny who took the floor.

"Time like this," Gunny said, "when folks are all gathered together to celebrate the accomplishments of someone, it is a tradition for the guest of honor to ... to say a few words to his friends and family.

"Now I know this is taking you a little bit by surprise, Jamaal," Gunny continued. "But do you have a few thoughts you could share with us?"

Jamaal was—no doubt about this—he was stunned.

Then Fredericks started it. Damn troublemaker, Jamaal thought. If he had a damn leg, Jamaal thought, he'd break it for him.

"Speech, speech, speech ...," Fredericks started chanting. By about the seventh or eighth time he said that word, everyone around the table had joined in. They were all laughing and smiling. He knew they were enjoying how embarrassed and uncomfortable he was feeling—putting him on the spot. And he also knew there wasn't anything but caring and affection in their hearts.

Jamaal raised his hands in a gesture of surrender and the chant died down. "I mean—you know—this whole evening was a complete surprise and I'm not prepared," he started.

"Stand up," the Rev said to him, in a loud whisper.

Jamaal looked over at the old man.

"Stand up," the old man mouthed the words very clearly.

Jamaal stood. He looked around the room. People—friends and family—smiling, looking expectantly at him. Good people. People who had stood by him. His throat tightened and his eyes threatened to start leaking tears, but he looked down, took a deep breath and got past that, at least for the moment.

Then Jamaal Thomas looked up, looked around the room again and felt the warmth of the feelings that surrounded him, and started talking.

"Everyone here knows that a year ago, I was released from prison. I was in a sorry state—no job, no home, no money to speak of and thousands of dollars in debt.

"But I got lucky. I run into this man. This old man. This bald-headed, gray-bearded, scrawny old man ..."

Jamaal took a quick look at the Rev to see if any of his digs were hitting home and the old man was just sitting there beaming at him.

"And Reverend Wright here, he started teaching me about some 'rules' to help me get out of the mess I was in. He introduced me to people—first to Gunny here, and then, one way or another, to the rest of you.

"Well, that's not quite right. Jennifer, Natalie, Jameela—you knew me before. Well, you knew someone who looked a lot like me, anyway. Someone who figured he could make a living on the streets. Get by. Play it cool. Hustle up some easy money. And that was the damn fool who spent a year being incarcerated. And that guy who looked like me, he ain't here anymore.

"Jennifer—I'm going to be forever in your debt. Thank you for being willing to take me in after I was released. You put a roof over my head. You helped save my life.

"Rev ..." Jamaal started. "Reverend Wright. Thank you for giving me that notebook and taking me around to learn the rules.

"You all need to understand—money can be just a huge problem for a man getting out of incarceration. You got these enormous bills and no job prospects. It's ... I mean, it's ... just awful.

"A year ago, I was fifteen thousand dollars in debt. As of about two weeks ago, I am debt-free. So, I can testify—the rules are powerful. They can help any man get back on track.

"Now I need to thank every one of you who helped me—taught me the rules—helped me get out of that deep hole.

"But—as important as the rules have been to me—there's been one more thing even more important and more powerful—helping me through this last, difficult year.

"And that's you—you people—who were willing to give this foolish young man a second chance. To give me the benefit of your wisdom. To give me encouragement.

"My story—it's like a fairy tale. I think about it and say to myself, 'man, that never could have happened.'

"But it did. It really did happen for me, and it wasn't anything crazy or some stoke of good luck.

"If a man has good principles—knows the rules and sticks with them ...

"If a man is willing to work hard—damn hard—and never give up ...

"If a man opens himself up and accepts the love and support of his family and his friends—his real friends—his buddies in the battles he's going to have to fight his way through ...

"If a man can do all of that—he can have a story to tell that'll be just as good as mine.

"Yeah, I've got a pretty good story to tell. But I promise, I will never forget that it was you—you people sitting here tonight, who made it possible. You gave my life direction. You gave me strength. You gave me hope. You believed in me."

Very slowly now, Jamaal looked around the room, making eye contact with every person, and he said, "Thank you. Thank you. Thank you."

Then Jamaal sat down.

Later That Night

The dishes were washed, and coffee and tea had been served and now almost all the guests had left. Jamaal had taken on dish-drying duty. He enjoyed being in the kitchen. As he worked, he could visit with the remaining guests. The kitchen is always the best place to be at a party, he thought.

Natalie, Jameela, and Jennifer were the last group to leave. Jennifer and Jameela already had their coats on and were waiting on the front porch while Jamaal was escorting Natalie through the foyer.

"Jamaal," Natalie said, as he helped her on with her jacket. "I was wondering if you'd like to come over for dinner next week?"

Jamaal blinked his eyes. Twice. Probably more than twice.

"Well, sure," he finally said. "Sure. That would be nice."

"Nothing fancy," she said. "Maybe you can bring something for dessert?"

"Of course," he said. He lowered his voice a bit and asked, "What's Jameela's favorite?"

"Oh," Natalie said. "Jameela has a sleepover with her friend, Sonia. It'll just be us two. You can surprise me."

Natalie stood on her tiptoes and kissed him on the cheek.

Jamaal opened the door and watched as the three most important women in his life went down the walk and turned right, toward Pacific Avenue.

When they were out of sight, Jamaal made one last tour of the parlor picking up a stray napkin he spotted and one more glass that needed to be washed. He completed his cleaning duties and turned to Gunny.

"Kitchen patrol complete, Gunny," he said. "Permission to turn in."

"Permission granted," Gunny said.

Jamaal took Gunny's hand and then embraced the former Marine in a "guy hug."

He stepped away. He looked at Gunny and then at the Rev who was also getting ready to leave. He looked at each of them again, straight in the eyes.

"Thank you," he said. Two words—and he spoke them as he had never said them before.

"Careful out there," Gunny said, as Jamaal and the Rev left the kitchen and went into the little hallway by the front door.

"You guys really surprised me," Jamaal said as he slipped into his jacket.

"That was the plan," the old man said. "We're proud of you, son. Damn proud. Wanted you to know it."

"Everyone—well, almost everyone you introduced me to—was here. For me." Jamaal shook his head. "Of course, Coach McKenzie …"

"She's a little busy running her camp program and getting ready for the season," the Rev said.

"I know," Jamaal said, "and I think they're going to the Final Four this year.

"Mr. Booker," Jamaal continued. "Did you guys …?"

"We invited him," the Rev said. "He declined, but he did ask about you—how you were doing. I gave him a good report, and he wished you good luck. Oh, and he said to remind you about one thing …"

"Wait—let me guess," Jamaal said, interrupting the old man. "The house always wins."

"I'm thinkin' that was a sucker bet," the Rev said. "You got it in one. 'Remind that boy, the house always wins,' that was what he said."

Jamaal reached for the doorknob. Then he stopped.

"Except," Jamaal said. "Except." He turned and looked at the old man. "Except for the rich dude. The richest man in New Babylon."

Jamaal was smiling at the old man.

"I've done everything you asked me to do," Jamaal said. "I worked my backside off. I followed the rules. I planned and I saved. Now when do I get to meet The Man?"

The old man was smiling, too.

"Turn around," the Rev said.

Jamaal turned his head and glanced backward. "There's nobody …" he started to say.

"Turn. Around," the old man repeated, saying the words slowly and spread apart, like he really meant it.

Jamaal turned around and looked at the old hall tree with its hooks, coats, hats, scarves … and its mirror.

Jamaal saw his own reflection in the mirror. "The richest man in New Babylon," he said, and smiled.

"Not quite," Jamaal said, shaking his head. But he kept looking at the mirror.

He smiled some more when he saw the reflection of the old man standing behind him, grinning. He thought about the dinner he just enjoyed. He thought about Jameela, who was such a beautiful child. He thought about having a date—yeah, that's what it was—a date with Natalie.

He looked at his face in the mirror again.

"Maybe," he said. "May. Be."

The Richest Man in New Babylon

Five Years Later

Daydreaming. Leaning on his broom out in front of the big old church on Pacific Avenue, Jamaal's mind drifted. Five years. Gunny had reminded him of the anniversary. Gunny kept track of that sort of thing.

Dontrelle Williams died in a shootout. Cops never figured out who was responsible—they just said it was a drug war. A lot of young men died that year. And a lot of innocent people died or got hurt.

Robbie Grayson found out about Dontrelle—how he and Jamaal had been friends a long time ago. He handled the funeral—didn't charge the family anything. Jamaal cried a bit. But seeing Dontrelle's mom and dad again, after so long, Jamaal began to understand a little about how a funeral could be a good thing, too. A celebration of some sort.

The Reverend Ezekiel Wright had come out of retirement for one day three years ago, to officiate at the wedding of Jamaal and Natalie Thomas. Jamaal and Natalie's friends had secretly organized themselves to give the couple one big wedding present: a trip to Disney World for Jamaal, Natalie and Jameela. Plus, a nice check to add to the family's emergency fund.

"Family gets bigger, savings got to get bigger," Gunny said.

"Pay yourself first," Jamaal said.

"Pay yourself first," Gunny said.

"Amen," the Rev said.

"Guess you ain't gone entirely back into retirement yet," Jamaal said.

Jamaal and Natalie were living in a cozy house on the same block as Gunny and Miss Booth. They currently rented the house with an "option to buy" contract on it that locked in the sale price. That would hold it for two years.

They were saving for a twenty percent down payment. If they didn't make it, they would be very, very close.

Jamaal now worked full time for Arnie Swann at Action Auto Parts. He was assistant branch manager at the downtown store. But after moving to the Pacific Avenue neighborhood, Jamaal realized that there really weren't any parts stores anywhere convenient for the neighborhood. He also spotted a shut-down filling station that had been expanded a couple times before it went out of business. He had brought it to Arnie's attention just last week.

"Light on inventory," Jamaal said, talking it over with Mr. Swann. "Focus on high turnover items and consumer stuff."

"Might work," Swann said. "More of a satellite branch, like the one on the South Side."

"Exactly," Jamaal said.

"Of course, we'd need a branch manager," Swann said. "Someone who really knows the neighborhood."

"Well," Jamaal said, "sometimes an enterprising young man has to create an opportunity. I remember someone told me that some time ago."

Swann laughed.

Jamaal didn't miss working at the packing plant. But he never missed lunch on Wednesdays with Arvin Parker. Jamaal had decided that he really liked Arvin. He enjoyed talking sports and cars with him. And Arvin had a sharp eye for talent, and he didn't mind if Jamaal recruited someone for the parts store. Arvin was all about helping people get ahead.

The biggest news in Jamaal's life had nothing to do with work. The biggest thing on his mind while he was standing out in front of the church, leaning on a broom on a fine fall day, was that he was going to be a father again. Natalie was pregnant, and she was looking so good, too. Jamaal shook his head. Who would have thought that? Pregnant was sexy. But it was, Jamaal was thinking. It was.

"Jamaal," a voice from right next to him woke Jamaal up.

A tall, skinny guy. Standing there. Sagging. For real sagging—not a fashion statement.

"Yeah?" Jamaal said.

He stared at the newcomer. The eyes, the mouth ... the hair. Kinda reddish, very light reddish. It took a while.

"Pink?" Jamaal finally said.

"Randall," the newcomer said. "I'm losing the street name. Gotta get out of the game. This city," he continued, "it's all changed. And I changed. I'm looking for a way out."

Jamaal looked at him. Still tall, even more skinny. But he wasn't looking so twitchy. Jamaal thought he was hearing some sincerity in his words.

"Randall," Jamaal said. "Randall?"

"Randall Jefferson," Randall said.

"How long you been out?" Jamaal said

"Got out yesterday. This is my first full day."

"And you're looking for me ... because ... ?"

"You made it. I heard that on the inside. I heard you figured stuff out, and you made it, and you're doin' good," Randall said. "I was thinking ... I was hoping ... maybe you could ... you know ... help me . . . you know ...?"

Jamaal looked Randall in the eyes. He was trying to see the truth in there. He knew he couldn't. It took time. There was always a chance. Things could go one way or another.

Jamaal made a decision.

"Damn," Jamaal said. "I thought I was going to have this whole afternoon to myself, and now you show up dragging your sorry ass into my life again. Damn."

He was smiling. Randall wasn't quite sure what Jamaal was up to, but he gave a half smile back.

"So, listen up," Jamaal said. "I got to find a friend of mine. Gotta talk something over. Meantime, I need someone to finish up my chores out here.

"Clean sweep," he said, handing Randall the broom and gesturing toward the steps and sidewalk. "Here on Pacific Avenue—we like to keep things neat.

"I'll be back in a few minutes, maybe bring my friend if I can find him. We can talk. Maybe get a cup of coffee."

He walked away, then turned and came back.

"There's rules you know," Jamaal said. "There's rules for how you get your life together after things have gone all to hell.

"There's folks you've got to meet. Can't begin to tell you how important that is, to get to know the right people.

"Then, you got to bust your ass. You gotta work and work and work. You gotta make mistakes and then recover from 'em. And work some more and …

"Damn," Jamaal said. "It's one hell of a lot of work. You think you can handle all that?"

Randall looked a little stunned. But he was listening hard. Jamaal thought there was a glint of determination in his eyes.

"Yeah," Randall said. "Yeah. I think I can handle all that."

"You follow the rules, meet the right people and work your butt off and maybe, just maybe, there will come a day when I can introduce you to the man with all the secrets of success."

"Who's that," Randall asked.

"The Richest Man in New Babylon," Jamaal said.

"What's his name?" Randall said. "When can I meet him?"

"In a while," Jamaal said. "Takes time. You gotta meet a lot of other people—learn the rules. It takes time.

"But first, you got some sweeping up to do."

The End

About the Author

Ridge Kennedy was born in Fort Smith, Arkansas. Then he moved to Philadelphia, Pennsylvania; Columbus, Ohio; Indianapolis, Indiana; Tokyo, Japan; Hatfield, Pennsylvania; Bangkok, Thailand; Fort Smith (again); Indianapolis (again); Cleveland, Ohio; and Mentor, Ohio. Then he went off to high school in New Hampshire.

No, he wasn't a military brat; his parents were in the newspaper business.

After majoring in speech and theatre in college and teaching theatre classes at Hiram College and Bucknell University, Ridge went into the family business, starting off as an intern at The Evansville Press. Over the next thirty years, he earned a living primarily as a writer: newspapers, technical writing, advertising, public relations and marketing. In the early days of the personal computer, he expanded his interests into technology. In the early 2000s his career veered into information technology; providing tech support and writing code instead of words.

Throughout his life, Ridge has also pursued an interest in folk music and dance. He is a song leader and dance caller. Google "yodeling square" and his name on YouTube for a glimpse of his alter ego in the folk arts world.

The Richest Man in New Babylon reflects another important area of interest for him; a deeply-felt desire to make the world a better place. Not just for him, his family and friends; but for people he doesn't know. Fellow Americans. Fellow residents of Planet Earth. Global warming, racism, income inequality, dictators and genocides—he worries about all that stuff, too.

His work on The Richest Man in New Babylon is a not-for-profit effort to help address the challenges faced by people, disproportionately men of color, who have been incarcerated in the United States. But the rules described in his book can be applied by anyone, anywhere, so that ticks the "income inequality" checkbox on Ridge's worry list, too.

For more information about Ridge and his ongoing projects, visit www.ridgekennedy.com. If you would like to support the effort to increase financial literacy for people who have been incarcerated, visit www.richestmaninnewbabylon.com.

401(k) Quiz Answers

1) In addition to saving for retirement, your 401(k) plan is also a good way to save for education expenses.

FALSE: If you withdraw money from a 401(k) plan before you are 59 ½ years old, you will have to pay a penalty (10 percent) and, additionally, pay the taxes due on the money withdrawn. There may be special hardship exemptions allowed for the penalty, but you will owe the taxes. A 401(k) plan is designed for retirement savings only; not emergencies, education or any other use.

2) Employers are required to match employee contributions up to a minimum of two percent.

FALSE: Employers MAY match your contributions, but they are not required to do so. If they match your contributions, it can be any amount they want to provide.

3) A 401(k) plan is "tax advantaged." This means that you don't have to pay any taxes on contributions to your 401(k) plan.

FALSE: You don't have to pay taxes on the income you contribute to your 401(k) when it is earned, but you will have to pay taxes when the money is withdrawn from the 401(k). Since your income may be lower when you have retired, you may end up paying less in taxes, but 401(k) income is not tax free.

4) If you take a job at a different company, you have to close your current 401(k) plan and enroll in a new one at your new company if it offers one.

FALSE: 401(k) plans are a big business in America and companies have made it easy to manage them. You can leave your money in your old employer's fund or you may have an option to move it into your new employer's fund (called a rollover). You should not cash in your 401(k) savings. You will be charged penalties and pay taxes.

5) All the money you contribute to your 401(k) plan is guaranteed to be yours to keep.

TRUE. You earned it. You keep it. But, if the investments you select go down in value, you could, theoretically, end up with less money than you put in.

6) All the money your employer contributes to your 401(k) plan is guaranteed to be yours to keep.

FALSE: Your employer is allowed to require your contributions to be "vested." For example, every year you may be guaranteed 20 percent of the employer contributions. So, after five years, you may be guaranteed all the employer contributions. If you leave the job earlier, you'll only get the amount that was "vested" at the time you left.

7) If you have a particular stock you want to buy, you can specify that in your 401(k) plan investments.

FALSE: Your 401(k) plan offers a limited number of investment options; typically, mutual funds, bond funds, real estate funds and similar groups of investments. You will have the opportunity to choose from the menu the fund offers. You won't be able to buy specific stocks.

8) If your employer's stock is included in your 401(k) options, you are required to allot twenty percent of your fund to it.

FALSE: Some 401(k) funds will include the employer's stock as an investment option, but there are no requirements that employees must choose it.

9) One good thing about a 401(k) plan is that there are no investment fees or additional costs.

FALSE: The people who run the 401(k) fund will charge fees, as will all the managers of the funds that are part of your investment portfolio. Regulations require 401(k) fund managers to disclose their fees. It's something employees should pay attention to; some funds have been known to charge much more than others.

10) It is sound financial advice to enroll in a 401(k) plan if your employer offers one with a matching contribution, and contribute as much as the employer is willing to match.

TRUE: If your employer is offering a match, you are "leaving money on the table" if you don't enroll and contribute at least that amount.

The Richest Man in New Babylon

Afterwords

This chapter covers a few additional ideas, principles, common concerns, questions, and topics that didn't fit into Jamaal's story. These are the footnotes—if you will—useful information that you can apply as needed.

Budgets

When I began teaching the money class, we started with a focus on budgeting. What is a budget? Why do you need a budget? How do you create a budget?

We discussed "needs" versus "wants." We talked about fixed expenses, variable expenses, discretionary spending and "liquidity." I brought in a laptop computer with a dedicated budget spreadsheet so that we could see exactly how a person's financial picture could change based on adding a little income here or cutting expenses there.

I learned that focusing on budgets was a mistake for three reasons.

First: Everyone has different financial needs and resources—there is no "one-size-fits-all" budget that you can share with a diverse group of people.

Second: Working as a group, it's extremely difficult to get people to agree about financial priorities. Discussions about needs and wants can be interesting and informative—and distracting. Dedicating a long section of the story to needs and wants seemed like an unnecessary diversion.

The third reason the story does not take a deep dive into budgets comes from my belief that, in the real world, most people don't use formal budgets. We have a pretty good idea of how much money we have coming in and what our big expenses are. We know roughly how much we have to pay for rent, utilities, phone service, food and transportation. We have a general understanding of where we stand and where we are going financially.

If you follow the rules—especially Rule Number 1 and Rule Number 2—the amount of money in your savings accounts gives you a good understanding of how you're doing. You can look at that to keep score.

Is it a good idea to create a detailed budget? Absolutely. When you sit down and write out all of your expenses, you have an opportunity to think about how you can try to reduce your costs and increase your income. Creating a budget will give you good ideas about how to plan for the future. And you can find lots of good information about budgeting in personal financial planning books and online.

But personally, I can't *maintain* a detailed budget. I can't keep it up to date. I tend to keep an eye on my bottom line: how much do I have in savings? How much is in my investment accounts? How can I save more/spend less? I focus on Rule Number 1 and Rule Number 2 and strictly obey Rule Number 4—never pay interest—to keep my finances in line. And I rely heavily on Rule Number 6—make it automatic—to keep things going in the right direction.

There are lots of different ways to approach budgets. For example, one woman I met while doing a money management class for a church group, was a strong advocate of "the envelope system". She used envelopes—each labeled with the kind of expense such as rent, transportation, insurance, food, clothing—and put money in each envelope. She embraced the process and told me that the envelope system helped her get out of student loan debt and put her financial life in order. Personally, I would never want to have that much cash around. Rule Number 6—keep your hands off your money—automate it. But the envelope system worked for her—proving that it's right for some people.

Budgets *are* important. For some of us, putting our budget in writing, using a phone app, or creating a computer spreadsheet may be the way to go. Online tools available with online banking or in third-party websites like Mint.com, allow you to create budgets, categorize expenses, and monitor everything in your financial life.

Other people—like me—we follow a few key indicators like our savings accounts. If we have a mortgage, how much equity do we have in our home?

Ultimately, a budget is very personal and something that each individual needs to consider and explore. You have to find out what works for you.

Debt

Words of wisdom:

> *Annual income twenty pounds, annual expenditure nineteen and six, result happiness. Annual income twenty pounds, annual expenditure twenty pounds ought and six, result misery.*
> — Charles Dickens, *David Copperfield*

The modern, consumer-driven, US economy has rationalized debt—made it seem "normal." A little debt is okay, we are told. Go ahead and charge it. Then the same voices say: "You're in good financial shape. So, you can take on a little more debt."

The voices saying that debt is okay are coming from people who want to sell us "stuff." They are not the voices of people who are sincerely looking out for our best interest.

I remember conversations with people involved with selling mortgages. They assured me, with straight faces, that I could "afford" to take on debt that was more than ten times my annual income, would cost me more in interest than the amount I was borrowing, and wouldn't be paid off for thirty years.

My life experience includes a fair amount of unnecessary credit card debt, years spent living paycheck to paycheck, and a personal bankruptcy. As a result, I suppose, debt has become a kind of phobia. Ultimately, I did take on mortgage debt, but with large down payments and the shortest terms I could afford. I constantly monitored the amount of money that was going toward interest (going to someone else) and that was being added to principal (my home equity—money going into my own pocket.) Here are some thoughts about debt for you to consider.

Debt for Automobiles?

Don't waste your money. Your vehicle is losing value all the time. It's *not* an investment; it's just another expense.

If you have a car loan, look at your statement and find out how much you are spending on interest compared to how much you are paying off on your loan. Now, imagine *all* that payment money going into your savings account. If you have a repair expense, you will have plenty of money to take care of it. You can maintain your vehicle in great condition. And when it comes time to upgrade your ride, you will have money—cash—to buy the best available used (pre-owned, as dealers say) vehicle you can afford. And the time will come when, if you want to, you can buy a new vehicle. And you won't have to go into debt to do it.

Just take that car payment and apply Rule Number 1, Rule Number 2, and Rule Number 4. Pay yourself first and put that "payment" money into your savings. You want to have more money? Spend less on cars or trucks or whatever you want to drive. And never pay interest.

What about leasing a car? Some financial advisors call a car lease a "fleece." You pay money every month and end up with nothing. Go online and look up "car lease" and "fleece" before you give away any more of your hard-earned money.

Debt for Education?

If you need to borrow money for school, that's always okay, right?

No! You need to be very, very careful.

Paying for job training seems like a good idea, right?

Be very, very careful.

Trade schools—for-profit institutes, online and for-profit universities that offer professional training programs—do *not* have a great track record. Any for-profit business in the education field is highly motivated to get you signed up as a student. These businesses earn money by getting you into debt. They know all the ins and outs of getting grants and loans, and they will find a way to help you "afford" their classes.

Unfortunately, these schools (businesses) do NOT have as much incentive to be sure their students (customers) complete their course of study. And they do NOT have a great reputation for placing all their students in the high-paying jobs they promise. But they DO have a great reputation for leaving students with lots and lots of debt.

Under current law, debt incurred through education loans cannot be discharged through bankruptcy. Recent changes in the bankruptcy laws make it virtually impossible to legally discharge student loan debt. So whatever debt you take on will follow you until it is paid off. If you miss payments, you'll be charged penalties and additional interest, so it can grow.

Before you sign anything, ask lots of questions.

What is the company's track record for placing students in jobs? Can you speak with graduates freely and quiz them—not just about their experience but also about their classmates' experience? What percentage of their students complete the program? What percentage of the students get jobs? If you are going to go into debt, you need to do a lot of serious research.

The people involved in admissions at for-profit schools and institutes are paid based on their ability to get you to sign up for their programs. Ask them, seriously: "If I was your brother, or your sister, would you recommend that I sign up?"

You need to be very skeptical about any claims that these businesses make about great jobs and successful career placements.

What about college loans?

Since the end of World War II, college education has always been considered to be a good investment. If you have to borrow money, it's okay, right?

Not any more—or at least not without careful consideration.

In some ways, colleges are acting just like businesses in today's consumer economy. They can assemble "financial aid packages" that are tailored to what you and/or your family expect to pay. Then they include scholarships (discounts), grants ("free" money from government programs), and loans to cover the rest of the cost.

Loans. That's where you have to be careful. How much can you reasonably expect to earn when/if you graduate. (Remember, if you don't graduate, you'll still have that loan debt—and you will not be able to escape it through bankruptcy.) Are you going to be able to afford loan payments? How much will they be? It's really important to think about these things before you agree to take on any debt.

My recommendation to families preparing to send children to college is to give serious consideration to attending a community college and living at home for the first two years. Then transfer to attend an in-state, public four-year school to get your bachelor's degree. Save your money and avoid debt. At that point in your education, when you have a bachelor's degree, you'll have a much better idea what your interests are and where your career is heading. In many fields, you will need to go on to get an advanced degree. Save money and avoid debt so you will have the financial flexibility, resources, and information to make wise decisions moving forward.

Debt—in general. Be very, very careful.

Plastic: Credit Cards and Debit Cards

Credit cards: a very complicated subject.

Credit cards are evil. Companies that issue credit cards make it easy to spend money. In fact, they make it much too easy to spend more money than you have. That's their business. They want you to spend more money than you have so that you start paying interest. Then, if they're lucky, you may miss a payment so they can charge you a penalty fee. And after that, they will charge interest on the penalty fee, interest on the balance you owe, and get you deeper into debt. Credit cards are evil.

Credit cards are great. With certain cards you can get two or three or even five percent of what you charge given back to you in cash "rewards." If you like to travel, you can get airline miles (if you want to get into the insanely complicated world of managing air miles). Credit cards allow you to go out with little or no cash—they reduce your risk of overspending just because you happen to have cash with you.

Credit cards are essential. More and more of the business we do is electronic. If you want to subscribe to an online service, buy something online, or rent a car, you have to have a credit card. If you use a "pay as you go" telephone service like TracFone (highly recommended for cheapskates!) you need a credit card.

Debit Cards. Debit cards are like credit cards but with a safety mechanism. With a debit card, you can only spend the money you have in the account linked to the card. You can't overspend—maybe. You have to be careful. Some banks and other institutions that issue debit cards may very well *allow you to overspend* and then charge you a penalty!

So, let's summarize what we know about debit and credit cards. They are kind of necessary evil for people in the United States today. You need them for some purposes. And they can be really useful. You can use them to save money, for example, at the grocery store where you can get rewards like cash back (a discount, in effect). But they are dangerous. They can let you get yourself deeper in debt and make it incredibly difficult to get out of debt.

If you get a credit or debit card, you need to understand what the rules for the card issuer are. You need to read the fine print or get someone on the phone (probably the best way to go) to tell you, in excruciating detail, exactly what happens if you overspend the limit on a debit card, for example or what happens if you don't make a payment on time. You need to understand how costly that can be.

And remember Rule Number 4. Never pay interest! If you get a credit card, you *must* pay it off in full every month. If you fail to do that—if you end up paying interest on your credit card—then you need to stop carrying it. Cut it up. Put it away under lock and key somewhere. Put it in a bag of water and store it in the back of your freezer. Don't use it until you get everything back under control.

Credit Reports and Credit Scores

Here's an overview of the world of credit reports and credit scores.

There are three big companies called credit bureaus that gather financial data and other information about everyone in the United States: EquiFax, TransUnion, and Experian. There are other, smaller companies in this business, but the big three are the ones that matter. They get information from stores, credit card companies, banks, utilities—just about every large business in the United States. The credit bureaus keep track of all the accounts a person has open, the amount owed, payments (and whether the payments were made on time) and more. When an account is closed, they keep the records for several years afterward, with information about whether the balance was paid in full and if payments were on time. The credit bureaus also track mortgages and car loans. They know what bank accounts people have and how much money is in them. They get court records so they have information about liens and bankruptcies. Their records include all the addresses where people have lived, places they have worked and names they may have used.

All of the data the credit bureaus collect is maintained in databases. That data, identified by a person's Social Security number and date of birth, is called a "credit file."

When a business wants to decide whether to extend credit to you, it may purchase a "credit report" or "credit score."

A credit report is a summary of the information in your credit file. It includes much of the information in your credit file but may not include everything.

A credit score is just a number. To simplify credit management decisions and help businesses make quicker decisions, an independent firm, Fair, Isaac and Company (now called FICO), came up with the credit score idea. A person's credit score is based on the information in the credit bureaus' credit files. The credit score summarizes all the credit file data with a number between 300 and 850. A score below 580 is considered poor. A score between 800 and 850 is considered excellent.

Payment history (paying bills on time), debt burden (the total amount owed), and length of credit history (maintaining an account with good payment history over a long time) are the three most important factors in determining a credit score.

Bottom line: big business has lots of data about our finances and ways to access it. But—when you apply the rules—credit reports and credit scores don't matter very much.

A poor credit score might increase the interest rate you pay for a consumer credit card. But since you follow Rule Number 4: Never pay interest—you don't care what the interest rate is. It's irrelevant.

For most of us, credit reports and credit scores are unimportant until the time you apply for a mortgage. That's when your credit score might have an impact on whether you can get a mortgage and what the interest rate will be.

Credit reports don't matter much—except for this: some employers in some states check a prospective employee's credit report. In all cases, the company is required to ask for your written permission to check your credit report. If the job involves working with money and the company's financial systems, companies in any state are allowed, with your permission, to check your credit report.

In some states, employers are not permitted to ask to review credit histories for non-financial jobs. Similarly, some states do not permit employers to ask about a prospective employee's criminal convictions (ban the box laws). So, there are a lot of state-to-state variations. You'll need to do your research to determine if your credit history can have an impact on your employment.

Since 2003, the three national credit bureaus have been required to disclose to individuals what information is in their credit files. As a result, the credit bureaus have created a website, freecreditreport.com, where you can, theoretically, see the information in your credit file.

Unfortunately, with an eye toward their bottom lines, the credit reporting agencies have done everything that they can to turn credit reports and credit scores into another way for them to earn profits. If you visit freecreditreport.com, you will see some information from one credit bureau. Then you'll be offered an opportunity to pay to see what the other credit bureaus say. The information you see on the website may or may not include all the data in your credit file. And the credit bureaus will use your contact information to try to sell you more "stuff" like credit monitoring services.

The best way to check your credit report and be sure that it's accurate is to contact each agency individually and request a credit report. And the easiest way to do this is—trust me on this—by mail. Go online and search for "annual credit report request form." (Include the quotation marks around the words.) You should find, among the first few results of your search, a link to a form on the Federal Trade Commission website (ftc.gov) you can print.

The form has the names of all three credit agencies on the top and a mailing address. It has boxes where you fill in your personal information, one letter at a time. You'll need to provide your Social Security number, date of birth, full name, and address. Toward the bottom of the form, there are check boxes that allow you to select which credit bureaus you want reports from. You can check all at once or get reports one at a time.

Doing all of this by mail takes more time. You have to wait for the mail to be delivered and the report to be sent back. But—it exposes you to less marketing and gets you a lot more information. If you need to correct anything on the report, do that by mail, too. The credit report you receive from the credit bureau will have instructions, and may even include a "dispute" form. Slow and steady is the best way to go. Search for "disputing errors on credit reports" on the ftc.gov website for instructions on how to correct errors, sample letters and more information.

Health Insurance

What's the first question people typically ask after congratulating a friend who has gotten a new job?

"Does it have benefits?" or words to that effect. And when people in the United States ask about "benefits," they are usually interested in just one thing: Does the job include health insurance?

For a complicated variety of reasons, the United States stands nearly alone among major, wealthy nations in its failure to provide health insurance or health care for all its citizens. Instead, we rely on a patchwork solution that leaves many people uncovered.

Many people get health insurance through their employers. In some cases, it may be available for the employee's family; sometimes just for the individual. Some people with low incomes qualify for Medicaid, but eligibility requirements vary widely from state to state. Older Americans may be eligible for Medicare. And in recent years, many Americans have obtained health insurance through plans available under the Affordable Care Act (a.k.a. Obamacare).

Even with all these options available, millions of Americans still go uninsured. When they are severely injured or very ill, they go to hospital emergency rooms for treatment. Or they simply go without any medical care and hope for the best.

When you think about your "assets," your heath and the health of your loved ones are just as important—even more important—than your money and your property. There are some people who think that insurance, particularly health insurance, is a waste of money unless it is used. They are wrong. The lack of health insurance makes people reluctant to seek medical care. They may become sicker as a result and, perhaps, die. Lack of health insurance may also leave huge medical bills and debt that may takes years to repay. Note that there may be special programs available from hospitals to help pay medical bills. Individuals, however, have to do the research and find them.

While there are limits as to what hospitals and bill collectors can do to collect medical debts, you have to do the research, understand your rights and work your way through a very challenging situation.

Having health insurance may provide you with easier access to good health care and financial peace of mind.

But be careful. Health insurance companies in the US are just like any other companies; they're in business to make a profit. You need to fully understand the cost of the insurance, what it covers, its limits, and any hidden costs. One key question to consider: What are the plan's "deductibles"? A deductible in an insurance plan is the amount of money you have to spend out of your own pocket before the insurance will pay for anything.

With automobile insurance, for example, you can pay more for the insurance, and have a $200 deductible. You pay the first $200 of any repair cost and then the insurance covers the rest. Or you can have a $500 deductible and pay less for the insurance. You agree to pay the first $500 for a repair. Then your insurance kicks in.

With health insurance, there are plans with deductibles that are only a few hundred dollars. You will pay out-of-pocket costs, but only up to the deductible amount. Even after you pay your deductible, your plan may not cover all of your medical costs. And the percentage of costs it covers may vary, based on the medical procedure.

You may also find very low cost, high deductible plans—sometimes referred to as catastrophic health insurance. They may have deductibles of $5,000 or more. You'll have to pay up to $5,000 before you get any benefit from the plan. But, if you have a serious illness, this kind of plan may save you from financial ruin.

Health insurance is important. It is also ridiculously complicated.

If you are offered insurance from your employer, it may be a good plan. But there is no guarantee of that. If you have to purchase health insurance from another source, take your time. Ask questions and keep asking questions until you fully understand what is covered and how much you will have to pay in case of a health care emergency.

Investing: One Rich Man's Strategy

Warren Buffet, famously one of the richest men in the world, has publicly described the estate plan that he is setting up for his wife when he passes away. He is quoted in various magazines as having said that he will leave ninety percent of the money invested in an S&P 500 stock index fund and the remaining ten percent in a money market account. This will provide her with long-term investment growth in a safe, inexpensive stock fund and give her access to cash whenever she needs it.

What's the lesson for the rest of us who are not world-famous, wealthy investors, who are just trying to make good decisions with our much, much smaller savings?

I think there are two big takeaways here. Number one, as Mr. Buffet suggests, if you want to make a safe, long-term investment, you can choose a stock index fund. The S&P 500 fund from Vanguard would be one good choice. Remember Rule Number 7: Investing is legalized gambling. Betting on the entire US economy is a reasonably safe bet. You won't get a huge win, but you will probably see slow, steady growth, marked with occasional hiccups.

Remember, though, the house always wins. The only question is: "How much?" Vanguard Funds have a well-deserved reputation for keeping their fees and costs low, and providing value to their customers.

Takeaway number two. Keep some of your money in a "liquid" fund where it is relatively easy to withdraw in case of an emergency expense. A number of online banks are offering high interest savings accounts at this writing. Look up "high interest savings" on the Internet.

If you want to do more research and find out more about the stock market and make wise investments—that's a personal choice. You can certainly seek out personal financial planners who will help you make good decisions. There is a cost involved so you need to be sure you understand how the financial advisors are being compensated.

The financial services industry has successfully made investing a central part of the American way of life. You can't put money in a savings account and earn five percent interest like people did in the 1950s and 60s. But, if you you're looking for a simple, relatively safe way to invest, you can bet on the entire American economy through a stock index fund.

Storefront Tax Preparation

Starting in January, you see small businesses open up offering tax preparation services. They will tell you that they are going to help you maximize your tax return and they will even offer to make loans to you based on your refund.

Be very, very, very, very careful.

If your income is less than a maximum yearly income ($69,000 for the 2019 tax year), you can file a federal tax return for free.

But even then, you have to be careful. Using the Federal Free File option can be tricky. The tax preparation companies don't necessarily make it easy for you. These companies have successfully lobbied Congress to prevent the IRS from providing free, easy tax payment/refund services for people with simple tax returns. They are businesses and will offer extra services and add-ons, and try to get you to pay for them.

If you go online, search for "IRS Free File" and you should find links to several firms offering free federal tax filing.

If you live in a state with a state income tax, you will have to get assistance with that separately. You can visit your state tax authority website to get information about how to do that. Some states have a free filing option, similar to the federal Free File program.

The easiest way to get tax assistance may be to look for an organization in your community that is running an IRS Volunteer Income Tax Assistance (VITA) Program.

No matter how you get your tax returns done, you need to be very careful and make sure you are doing it completely legally. Report all your income—especially any "1099" income.

What is 1099 income? Employers are legally required to report any wages, tips and other compensation when they pay someone $600 or more in a calendar year. Employers ask you to fill out a W-2 form that has your Social Security number and your address. They report the income to the Internal Revenue Service (IRS) by issuing a 1099-MISC form. You receive a paper form from the employer at the end of the tax year, and the data is also sent to the IRS.

You need to be sure that all 1099 income is reported and you need to be sure that any deductions you claim are legitimate. Tax preparation and processing by the IRS is highly automated. If you make a mistake—not reporting 1099 income, for example—the IRS computers will probably catch it. If you claim a dependent and someone else claims the same dependent, the computers will catch that, also.

Today, people with low incomes are far more likely than very wealthy people to have their returns flagged for audits by the IRS because so much of what the IRS is doing today is automated.

So—be careful. Be aware that you may be entitled to free tax services. Don't waste money on fees or interest for "advances" on your tax refund. And don't make the mistake of claiming a dependent that someone else may claim or fail to report income from a 1099-MISC form.

Taxes in General

With a little planning, you won't have any problems with owing money for taxes.

If you are earning wages from an employer who is withholding taxes, you are all set, and will probably get a tax refund.

If you are earning money as a contractor (driving for a ride-sharing service or doing delivery work, for example), you may need to make quarterly tax deposits yourself. You are basically running a small business with yourself as your only employee. So, you need to learn about "safe harbor" rules to be sure you don't incur any penalties or interest charges.

Here are three rules for understanding Federal taxes:

1: All income is taxable—unless specifically exempted.

2: Nothing is deductible—unless specifically allowed.

3: Tax laws are illogical—they are a messy collection of rules, regulations, requirements and special exceptions passed by Congress at different times for different reasons.

Some people have a negative attitude towards paying taxes. Don't. Think of taxes as the price you pay for being successful, earning money, and enjoying the benefits of living in a great country.

And don't worry about taxes if you have an opportunity to work overtime. The withholding tax will only be a small percentage of your increased income; never all of it.

Depending on your total income, it's quite possible you'll get some or most of the money withheld back as a tax refund when you file your tax return.

There's another benefit to paying taxes. If you apply for a mortgage, for example, your tax returns provide mortgage lenders with the information they need to approve the loan.

Credit Unions vs. Banks

Everyone needs to be "banked." You need access to state-of-the-art, online banking services, access to automated teller machines (ATMs), savings and checking accounts—and you need to get all of this at a fair price.

Before you open a bank account at the nearest commercial bank, you owe it to yourself to consider all your banking options—especially this one: bank or credit union?

Credit unions are non-profit organizations created to serve their members. In order to use a credit union, you have to be a member. Sometimes, that means you have to be an employee at a specific company or a relative of an employee. But credit unions can have other membership criteria such as where you live or membership in some other organization.

For one of the biggest credit unions, Consumers Credit Union, you are "required" to join the Consumers Cooperative Association (for a one-time, $5 fee). That will qualify you to become a member and join the Consumers Credit Union. Or, consider the nation's biggest credit union. Anyone who is serving or has served in any US military branch, or worked for the federal government (or is a relative of any of those people) is eligible to belong to the Navy Federal Credit Union.

A large, modern credit union (CU) offers all the same services as large banks. The overall costs for a credit union are lower. The major disadvantage of credit unions is that they typically have fewer in-person branches. To make up for that, large CUs have very large networks of fee-free ATMs and they cooperate with other CUs to provide in-person "shared branch" services.

Banks are for-profit businesses. They have a responsibility to provide a financial return to their shareholders. As a result, they may have higher fees for some services, higher interest rates for loans, higher minimum deposit requirements, charges for checks and overall, be more expensive than a comparable credit union.

The big advantage of banks: lots of branches where you can speak to someone in person.

Do your research. Look up credit unions and banks on-line. Personally, I have been a very satisfied credit union member for more than forty years. But, I have also worked with banks—specifically for mortgages and high interest-earning, online savings accounts.

The financial services industry in the United States is huge and highly profitable. Be a smart consumer (a cheapskate) and explore all your options when it's time to "get banked."

Yes! Yes! Yes! Be a Cheapskate!

You work hard for your money. Don't let people take it away from you by selling you "stuff" you don't need. Fashion trends and fads; keeping up with the Jones; these behaviors violate Rule Number 2. Businesses are advertising, marketing, using social media, and paying influencers—just to try to entice you to buy stuff that you don't really need. Resist!

Remember Rule Number 2: If you want to have more money, spend less!

If you go online, you can find lots of people and websites with advice on ways to do more with less and ultimately spend less money. Search for terms like "frugal living," "minimalism," and "cheapskate." Poke around. You'll find a lot of ideas and many that you may want to use.

If you want to be kind to the earth and to your pocketbook, follow the 4Rs: Refill, Reuse, Repair, and Recycle.

Refill. This involves some logistics and setting up systems, but it's an effective way to save money. With a lot of things you use, you want to have them in small, convenient sized containers. When you run out, do you buy another small convenient sized container? A lot of the things we use such as dish washing soap, cooking oil, rice, glass cleaner, and similar products are available in large, less costly refill sizes. Some stores and co-ops encourage their customers to bring in containers, have them weighed, and then sell bulk items based on the actual weight of the product. Refilling is a good way to save money and reduce waste.

Reuse. Whenever you have something that is still useful—the clothing your kids grow out of or the vase some flowers came in—even the packaging a product comes in—is there a way to reuse it? I keep cardboard boxes (recycled) where I put things I'm not using anymore, but that could be useful for someone else. These include kitchen items and clothing. When a box gets filled, I take it to a nearby Salvation Army thrift store. Some of the other things I collect are clever boxes, gift bags, packaging materials and even the occasional bit of furniture or construction material I pick up by the side of the road on trash pick-up day. I keep them and reuse them.

Repair. This is more difficult in the era of integrated circuits and miniature electronics, but there are still times when you can fix an expensive piece of gear with a soldering iron. Tables and chairs? With a little glue and care, things that seem to be broken can be fixed and returned to "as good as new" condition. Lamps and other small appliances can be repaired. If a washing machine or dryer breaks down—there is probably a video on YouTube that will explain exactly how to fix it. With a few tools, the replacement parts you need to buy, and some ingenuity, you can probably do the repair yourself. And be sure you have a small sewing kit. Remember the old saying: "A stitch in time saves nine." A small repair can save much more than nine stitches. It can save you real money.

Recycle. Take some time and figure out what kinds of plastic are in fact recyclable and make sure you get them into the proper containers. If you can, take up composting. Be resource respectful. What does recycling have to do with your financial well-being? It's all part of a bigger picture. Caring about the resources and the future of the planet: that's one more good thing you can do for yourself and your family, and protect the environment while you're doing it.

So be a cheapskate. Visit websites dedicated to the idea of finding less expensive ways to do things. You'll find hundreds of ways to follow Rule Number 2! If you want to have more money, spend less.

Parting Words

As Gunny says, early in Jamaal's story, surviving in the modern American economy is like going to war. You have enemies everywhere; enemies who want to take away your hard-earned money.

Sometimes the attempts to rob you are as obvious as a street corner mugging. Rent-to-buy stores. Payday loans. Credit card debt. The people running these businesses are upfront about it. They make you sign paperwork that tells you: "this is a stick up." You have no excuses; you know you're getting robbed.

And there are so many more, sneakier, devious ways that people are trying to separate you from your money.

There are hidden fees for services, penalties and interest if you miss a payment, charges for this, that, and the other. And they all add up.

Then manufacturers and marketers bombard you with advertising, celebrity endorsements, and social media influence to encourage, urge, move, and motivate you—to give your money away. They want you to feel ashamed because you don't have "this" or embarrassed because your "that" is two years old. Or they try to make you feel guilty because you are not buying something for your spouse or children. They spend huge amounts of money on research to try to find the buttons they can push—to separate you from your money.

Seriously—it's a war. You, all by yourself, against all the forces of American consumerism.

Be strong. Fight back. Follow the rules. Be a cheapskate. Stop worrying about money. Put yourself on the road to financial security.

Resources

First, be careful. The Internet is filled with financial misinformation, special offers and straight-up scams. If it sounds too good to be true, it usually is. Following are a few resources you can trust.

Internal Revenue Service: www.irs.gov Information about free tax filing (freefile), volunteer tax assistance (VITA), and help with any other tax related questions.

Federal Trade Commission: www.ftc.gov and www.consumer.ftc.gov Information about credit reports, credit freezes, and all things credit related. Also home of the "do-not-call" list, information about preventing identity theft, and other helpful personal finance information.

Personal Finance Writers and Books: Michelle Singletary writes for *The Washington Post* and has written many smart, thoughtful, and practical books. Check her books in your local public library. Same goes for **Suze Ormond**, who also has a website with a lot of resources. **Dave Ramsey**'s books are good; but his website is too interested in selling stuff, I think. For one book on investing, check out **A Random Walk Down Wall Street** by **Burton G. Malkiel**. Straight talk advocating index funds, diversification and patience.

Consumer's Cooperative Credit Union: A CU you can definitely qualify to join. There's a $5 membership fee.

Navy Federal Credit Union: The biggest credit union in the US by a huge margin. Members must have some connection to military or government service. If you have a relative who qualifies, you can encourage him/her to join and then you can qualify as a relative of a member. Your relative will thank you for years to come.

Affinity Federal Credit Union: My home team. I weaseled a membership about four decades ago when it was the AT&T Employees Federal Credit Union. Membership is focused in and around New Jersey.

www.mint.com: Owned by Intuit, a big tax prep and accounting software company. Mint.com allows you to link all your credit union, bank, credit card, mortgage, 401(k), and investment accounts in one place. You can track expenditures, create budgets and more. You can know where you stand in real time. Free. Just ignore the offers to sell you stuff.

Acknowledgments

This book was inspired by the men I met leading The Money Class at Integrity House in Newark, NJ. Their life experience opened my eyes to the extraordinary financial challenges facing men and women who have been incarcerated. "The system," as it is currently configured, is designed to punish them further and encourage them to re-offend. Our nation needs to do much, much better.

Thanks to the leadership at Urban Renewal, Inc., Operators of a halfway house in Newark, NJ, who arranged for me to lead several classes using a draft copy of the book, and the readers there who gave me feedback. Thank you, Boris Franklin, author, poet and motivational speaker, who reviewed the story and language, and helped make it more realistic.

My work as a writer for the New Jersey Society of Certified Public Accountants helped inform this book. I learned about the modern principles and practice of personal financial planning while working with personal financial planning experts on feature stories and news releases. Along the way, I was introduced to George Clason's book, *The Richest Man in Babylon*. In my work at the Society, I discovered that CPAs tend to be very nice people who are generous with their time, and that they are great proofreaders.

Special thanks to Don Meyer, my communications department boss when I worked at the Society, who recently helped me get in touch with some of my advance readers from the CPA world; and to Joe Middleton, my IT department boss, who was one of the very early readers of this book.

Advance readers: Jean Abbott, Melissa Dardani, Jeanne Felfe, Michael La Ronn, Ken Shapiro, Anna Schubarth and Taneisha Spall. Thank you all for your time, your feedback and recommendations for improvements. Thank you, thank you, thank you.

And extra special thanks to Damon Freeman and Chrissy at Damonza.com who donated the cover design to the project, and to Jeanne Felfe who donated her editorial review.

Grateful thanks to my Foster brother, Irv, who was a first listener and has been consistently encouraging and supportive of this project.

Finally, most special thanks to Jane, for her trust and support in navigating our personal financial journey and for being, quite simply, the best person I know.

Reviews & Feedback

Dear Reader,

Your feedback is important and valuable! We need it!

If you liked this book and felt it was useful, your responses will help us spread the word and encourage other people and classes to use it.

If you found problems with the book or have suggestions for making it better, please tell us about your concerns and recommendations. Our goal is to make the book as useful as possible for future readers, and you can help us do just that.

If you purchased your book online, please leave a rating and review on the bookstore website. If you're in a class with Internet access, you can send a review by e-mail to us at reviews@richestmaninnewbabylon.com

If you don't have Internet access, please write a review or offer comments below and arrange to have your feedback sent as a scanned image or .pdf to reviews@richestmaninnewbabylon.com.

Thank you. Thank you very much. Ridge

- -

What did you like?

Suggestions for improvements?

Made in the USA
Middletown, DE
19 July 2023

35446923R00130